Onward Christian Sailors

Adventures of a Priest in the Royal Navy

Michael Wishart

First published by Michael Wishart 2021
Copyright © Michael Wishart 2021
The moral right of the author has been asserted.
Some names have been changed.
Cover design Bogna Zwegrodzka
ISBN: 9798757541150

This book is dedicated to Jeannetta, Sarah, Mary and John who bore the brunt of the separations.

Also, to the Chaplains of the Royal Navy, particularly those with whom I served. They were always kind to me even when I got it wrong which was, I believe, most of the time.

Contents

Foreword

Chaplains in the Royal Navy are extraordinary people, in its most literal sense: they are not ordinary. As the only members of HM Armed Forces who hold no rank, as priests who minister to all faiths and none, as providers of spiritual support for all roles and all ranks, as clergymen who move from ship to ship and unit to unit with an ever-changing array of parishioners, as Servicemen who also act as entertainment officer, education officer and negotiator for some who step out of line, they are not ordinary. All members of the Naval Service can remember the Chaplains with whom they have served, and all of them have special qualities that both set them apart from the rest of us and make them an essential and highly valued element of the Service.

In this light-hearted but open and deeply personal account of his four-year tour as a priest in the Royal Navy, Michael shares with us not only the best of times but also those when things were less than rosy. I have heard many reasons for men and women wanting to join the Armed Forces, but Michael is the first to attribute it to accident and anger. Both might, at first sight, seem somewhat negative, or at least liable to subsequent regret, yet it is clear throughout the book that Michael's approach was unfailingly positive and forward looking.

Every Service career starts with training. Michael's took place at Dartmouth and clearly showed that the 'accident and anger' had rapidly been replaced by enthusiasm, resilience, and a strong sense of humour.

The curate from Swansea was now ready for the Naval Service. Whether by accident or design, Michael began his career with the Royal Marines. Although his wish was to go to sea, I suspect that the move to the Corps was 'by design', in light of those senior Chaplains whom he met during the joining process, but I have no proof. Nevertheless, the result was a happy one for the Corps who could welcome another distinctive character as one of its Chaplains. It is clear from his account that Michael played a full and active part in all aspects of 40 Commando's varied programme, including street lining for the Silver Jubilee, a damp tent on Salisbury Plain, firefighting in Glasgow and an amphibious landing in Sardinia, but the sea beckoned.

Michael's eloquent account of his semi-nomadic existence ministering in, and to, a succession of frigates is a vibrant series of snapshots of the Royal Navy's tasks and geographic reach at that time. The hallowed tradition of First Night Cocktail Parties on arrival in overseas ports and the Runs Ashore of subsequent days paint a kaleidoscopic picture of British maritime presence and allied co-operation from the Americas to the Black Sea and the Arctic to the Azores. Venice provides a striking contrast to Constanta and Gibraltar to Antwerp.

Throughout his story, Michael's humanity and care for 'his' Sailors and Royal Marines shine through. To him, acts of kindness are the duty of a Chaplain and there are innumerable examples of pastoral care that the chain of command would recognise and warmly applaud. There are also some where the Run Ashore had lasted too long and 'the Bish' stepped forward to guard his flock from the scrutiny of, and subsequent retribution by, the chain of command. There are also instances that required all of

Michael's evident negotiating skills. In every case, his instincts to support the welfare and long-term well-being of those with whom he served are very clear, even when this led him to disagree with those in command.

Although Michael's wife, Jeannetta, and his three children make only fleeting appearances in the script, they are ever present throughout the story, as are spouses and children in every Service family. Parting from them to go on deployment or operations is a struggle; homecoming is euphoric. On each occasion, the unspoken question is whether to remain in the Services or leave. For Michael and his family, this thread runs through all the 4 years, in exactly the same way.

And then, it's over. Homeward bound, and civilian life beckons. In Michael's case this move was back home to South Wales, with the separation from the sea soothed by the enduring Naval link of the chaplaincy at *HMS Cambria*, the South Wales Division of the Royal Naval Reserve.

Those who have served in the Royal Navy and Royal Marines, and their families, will readily recognise the ships, the units, the adventures, the highs and the lows – but above all the eternal and indispensable camaraderie. Those who have not served have here a vivid picture, not of strategy or tactics, not of war or peace, but of the men and women in uniform and of a series of essentially human episodes of life in one of Her Majesty's Armed Forces, seen through the eyes of an extraordinary Royal Navy officer.

Rob Fulton
(Lt. Gen.Sir Robert Fulton KBE; KStJ)
October 2021

Prologue

It was never my intention to join the Royal Navy as a chaplain. It never occurred to me and it came about largely by accident and by anger.

The 'accident' was my seeing a wartime TV documentary in which there was no dialogue. It was silent apart from background music and a narrator. The part that really impressed me showed a kamikaze strike on a US aircraft carrier that had wooden decks. The chaos was enormous. There were fire hoses snaking all over the decks; there were fires raging and sailors rushing everywhere.

In the midst of this chaos there was a wounded sailor on a stretcher. He was being comforted by the ship's chaplain who had a Cross painted on on his helmet. You couldn't hear what he was saying, but in the midst of this desperate situation there was a moment of calm spiritual help for an individual sailor in great distress and that impressed me hugely. The 'anger' came years later in the summer of 1975 when I was serving as a curate on a council estate in Swansea. A number of colleagues and I had re-formed what was euphemistically called the 'Junior Clergy Association' which met once a month at St James' Church Hall in Sketty, Swansea. As we were the largest number of men to be ordained in the history of the diocese, we were encouraged to revitalise the Association which had largely become a time of tea, biscuits and gossip for the senior clergy.

We set about organising a programme with an extensive variety of speakers, ranging from the retired Archbishop of Canterbury, Dr Michael Ramsey, to those of humbler ministries. The programme took a great deal of work to set up and everyone was looking forward to it. The parish couldn't afford to give me a telephone and my incumbent, Hayden Moses, called at the house one day and said that the bishop's secretary had telephoned him with a message: the bishop wanted to see me and the other members of the committee who had organised the junior clergy programme. The bishop lived at Ely Tower in Brecon and we were instructed to report to him on a given date and time. It sounded quite ominous.

When we arrived, we weren't asked to sit down. The bishop just looked at us and said, 'It will not happen.'

None of us knew what he was talking about and I said 'Father, I'm sorry, but what will not happen?'

He replied, 'This program that you've devised.' I asked why and he said: 'I don't have to give you a reason, but it will stop!'

There was nothing for us to say. We looked at one another and left. There was a stunned silence all the way back to the cars. Once we got back to the car park we began to ask questions but could come up with no answers. The upshot was that everyone vowed to leave the diocese because we'd been stifled for no good reason. As Secretary, I had to write to all the people who had agreed to take part in our programme of events and apologise for wasting their time. It was a humiliating experience.

One of the people to whom I wrote was the Chaplain

of the Fleet, Ven. Chandos Morgan. He had been due to send a naval chaplain to us to take part in a symposium on chaplaincies. The Chaplain of the Fleet wrote back to me and said that if I was interested in the role of a naval chaplain to visit him for a chat. I had seen my future within the parish ministry, so I mulled over the question: did I really want to go to London to learn about a job in which I had little interest? But then I thought, what the hell? Why not?

I wrote back expressing my interest in the role and, within a few days, received a rail warrant. I caught a train to London and a taxi to Theobalds Road where part of the Ministry of Defence was located. Before I met the Chaplain of Fleet, I was interviewed by the staff chaplain, Noel Jones.

He told me, 'The Chaplain of the Fleet will say one of three things. Firstly, that he does not think that you are right material; secondly, you're just a sort of chap we are looking for; or thirdly, that you are the right sort of chap, but you need more experience.'

To my astonishment, he said that I was the right sort of chap and he wondered when I could start. It was very flattering. I later I found out that they were desperately short of men, so I wasn't that exceptional!

On returning home I had to approach my bishop for his permission to leave because the Chaplain of the Fleet could not make an offer without his agreement.

I arranged to meet the bishop on one of his weekly visits to Swansea, ironically at St James' Hall, and told him what had taken place. I explained that I had chaplaincy work in mind as the next step in my ministry. He seemed relieved and offered no opposition to the idea at all, so the way ahead was clear. I then had to discuss it with my wife, Jeannetta, and my vicar, both of whom knew what had taken place earlier and had been encouraging to me.

Nevertheless, I agonized over the whole thing because I had never really thought much about chaplaincy work. I just wanted to be an ordinary parish priest, but I had to make my mind up. One of the things that impressed me most about naval chaplaincy was that naval chaplains do not have a rank, unlike the British Army or the RAF. It all stems from the changes in the naval command structure in 1910 when the then Second Sea Lord tried to foist rank onto the Chaplain's Branch, but the then Chaplain of the Fleet threatened to resign and to encourage all the chaplains to do the same.

At the time, he explained: 'We are priests of the Church and as such we do not need rank.'

It was true then, and it is true to this day, despite some chaplains angling for it. The suggestion of rank was swiftly quashed, but it was agreed, as a compromise, that chaplains would accept officer status and live in the wardroom. Of course, I didn't know that then. After much prayer and deliberation, I wrote to the Chaplain of the Fleet and accepted his offer. And so began an adventure and a love affair with the Royal Navy that continues to this day.

Occasionally, in these recollections, I have used a pseudonym to save someone personal embarrassment. These events happened a long time ago, so, although I have tried to write chronologically, memory being what it is, I could be out by the odd day here and there. Mea culpa!

Chapter One

A New World Opens Up at Lympstone

Having accepted the Chaplain of the Fleet's initial invitation for a chat, the first thing was to allow the wider Navy to have a look at me. So, not many days later another letter arrived from the Chaplain of the Fleet asking me to go to Portsmouth for an 'acquaint' visit. This was a three-day visit to allow the Navy to look at me and I at it. I was sent a rail warrant and journeyed to Portsmouth Harbour Station where I was met by the chaplain of St Ann's Church, David Evans. He took me to the wardroom and, after finding my cabin and showing me around the public bits of the building, he left for home, telling me that I could have a half pint of beer on his number. I didn't know what he was talking about but I was extremely overawed by my surroundings.

There were several old sofas and large oil paintings of famous sea battles and people in uniform. I felt very alone and hadn't a clue as to what I should be doing. Then in walked a man in a roll necked sweater. He excused his rig to the officer of the day and when he saw me said, 'Hello. Who are you?' I told him and he introduced himself as Gwyndaf Hughes, chaplain of *HMS Nelson* the main barracks. He was going out for the evening with friends but he bought me a drink and we talked. Eventually, he said 'Excuse me a moment' and left. When he returned he had changed into collar and tie and said, 'It's more important that I spend the evening with you.' I will be eternally grateful for his kindness and company for I learned much from the short time together. The next few days was spent meeting various people from the dockyard admiral to sailors in ships (incidentally, one is never 'on' a ship but 'in'. The same way one is never 'on' a house! I thought I'd just mention it in passing).

It was a whirlwind time and I loved it. Just before leaving the little office behind St Ann's, David Evans then asked if I still wanted to join. Assuring him that I did, I caught the train home.

It was necessary for me to have a medical. Why it could not have been done in Portsmouth is beyond me so, a week or so later, it was back to London and the Empress Building, another part of the Ministry of Defence, to see the doctors. I thought that this was as far as I would go because I had suffered a burst ulcer a few years earlier and my stomach was never the best. The navy takes ulcers very seriously, but I provided them with the full details and explained that it didn't bother me, so that particular box was ticked, and I passed. Then it was back to the parish and to wait. The next step was to approach the bishop for permission to leave and he seemed to be relieved at my request and had no objection to it whatsoever. I informed my incumbent and the members of the parish of my intentions and in due course received a letter from the naval secretary informing me of my appointment as assistant chaplain to the Commando Training Centre, Royal Marines at Lympstone. A correspondence began with the chaplain, Raymond Roberts, a Welshman from Newport. I did not know it then, but this was to develop into a lifelong friendship.

On 26 April, 1976, I left the parish and drove across the Severn Bridge and down through the West Country to the turn-off at Exeter. I took the road to Exmouth, eventually coming to the village of Lympstone. On the outskirts of the village is the Commando Training Centre, Royal Marines. To say that I was apprehensive is an understatement. Military establishments were completely outside my experience. I slowed the car as I approached the guardroom and wound down the window.

The corporal of the guard came over and said: 'Can I help you sir?'

'I hope so,' I replied, 'I've come to join the Royal Navy.'

A puzzled expression crossed his features. 'Can't join the Royal Navy here sir. You have to join at Portsmouth, Plymouth or Chatham.'

I pulled my letter of appointment out of my pocket and handed it to him. That's when his expression altered. He stood back, snapped a salute, called over one of the marines and said: 'Take this officer to the officers' mess. Welcome to Lympstone, sir.'

The marine duly showed me the way to the mess and then I went to park my car at the rear entrance. I walked back along the corridor until I came to a reception desk and saw a steward.

I said: 'Good afternoon, I'm looking for the Reverend Raymond Roberts.'

As I spoke, a clergyman crossed from one side of the corridor to the other and I said, 'Mr Roberts?'

He looked at me and said, 'Yes.'

'I'm Michael Wishart and I've come to join the Royal Navy.'

He looked me up and down with an imperious look as if I was something the cat had dragged in and said: 'Do you normally go round in clothes like that?'

'I do when I'm just driving a car.'

It was not the most auspicious beginning, but it got better. Raymond took me to the main desk to get me signed in and got all my documents sorted out before escorting me to my cabin where we sat down and talked. It was the beginning of a very long and at times fraught friendship, but it has lasted down the years. Raymond was a good tutor, he introduced me to all aspects of life in the Royal Navy. A few days later we went down to *HMS Drake* in Plymouth so that I could get kitted out in the main stores. I also met other chaplains in the naval base church of St Nicholas who made me most welcome.

The other task I had to complete quickly was obtaining a married quarter so that I could move my family down. It only took a day or so and we were assigned a fully-furnished quarter in Lympstone village.

Our furniture went into storage with friends and family in preparation for the move. The girls were small: Sarah was three-and-a-half years old, while Mary was just eighteen months old. I travelled back to Swansea and after packing the car, and, bidding a tearful farewell to my mother, we set off for a complete change in our lives. It might have been interpreted as a bad omen, but Mary cried the whole way there. I was so glad that I had gone into Mothercare in Exeter and bought a Wendy House which I had erected in the sitting room in the quarter. It pacified Mary and delighted Sarah as we settled into our new surroundings.

All members of the armed services have to go through an initial period of training and the Royal Navy is no exception. Ratings go to *HMS Raleigh* for a period of twenty-six weeks to be taught the ways of the navy. Naval officers have similar but more intense training at the Britannia Royal Naval College, Dartmouth. Naval officers have a lengthy period at Dartmouth covering all aspects of the work that they hope to undertake, whereas specialised people like chaplains, doctors, dentists, instructor officers and nursing sisters, who are already trained, are destined for a limited course which is a sort of navalisation process.

When I arrived at Lympstone, Ray Roberts outlined the programme that I would undertake over the next few months, culminating in the commando course scheduled for September. He also informed me that I was to go to Dartmouth for a period of one month to undergo this navalisation. It was to be the first of many separations from my wife and the children.

I packed my trunk, drew a rail warrant and headed off to Dartmouth on the appointed day and reported to the course officer at Hawk Division. The college is a very imposing building constructed on a hill overlooking the town of Dartmouth, the River Dart and its estuary. It's a beautiful part of Devon and the site was carefully selected in the early twentieth century to create an imposing building outside and within. The college routines are designed for the instruction of cadet officers from their very first day until their last.

When I reported for the scheduled four weeks' training, I was informed that it had been reduced to two weeks because there was nobody else there who was scheduled for a month's training. The two weeks proved to be exhausting enough though. I thoroughly enjoyed them and it ranged from lectures on the 'Red Threat' to boat drills. Sometimes it didn't feel like much fun when I had to charge from a boat drill at Sand Quay up the long flights of steps to my cabin in Hawk Division to change in order to attend a lecture – and you wouldn't dare be late!

We were up early in the morning to help with the cleaning, including the 'heads' (bathrooms and toilets) and did not get to bed until late at night. Despite the long days, it was great fun and a good training for shipboard life.

Part of the course was a visit to *HMS Raleigh* for damage control training which involved going into a specially-created section of a ship mounted on gimbals. After changing into suitable overalls, on entering, we found ourselves in a replica compartment of a ship. The training staff then introduced us to various aspects of damage control to make our day difficult. We combatted flooding under emergency lighting while the compartment rolled back and forth with water submerging us from time to time; all the while you were trying to get a mattress or a splinter box over the hole to stem the flooding. One solution was for someone to climb a vertical ladder and lower down a pump in order to pump the water up and over the side.

Safety was always the priority. In the event of an emergency the compartment could be emptied of water by the staff hitting a button. The water would then cascade out through the large openings in the deck which were covered by metal grilles. We also underwent firefighting training at *HMS Phoenix* which involved getting into a Fearnought suit and going into a compartment where there was a fire. It was an interesting experience. You could be within a few feet of a fire and not see it but feel it with the lobes of your ears which are the most sensitive part of the body. Ear lobes pick up heat very, very quickly, and even in a heat resistant suit you could feel it. We were also taught that if you are entering a compartment where there is a fire, and you can't see it, use the back of your hand to tap the metal bulkheads to feel whether it's getting hotter. I was literally within two feet of the simulated fire before I could see it because of the dense smoke.

Another aspect of the course was helicopter training. There was a small helicopter landing pad on a hill above the college and that's where the training session took place. It involved being winched up into a Wasp helicopter. Although I don't have a head for heights, I found it quite exhilarating; at the same time, I was terrified. It wouldn't bother me now, but it did then. I had walked into a military way of life from a civilian parish and it was a new experience for me and very frightening, but as the old saying goes, 'If you can't stand a joke, you shouldn't have joined up!'

One morning I was summoned by the course officer and told to go and prepare to join a group of cadet officers for a weekend expedition of boat handling and map reading up the River Dart. We went in a Huntress motor boat which had twin engines and was six berths. It was used extensively for the boat training at the college and by ships of the fleet. Since we were away for the weekend, I had to organise a short service. It comprised a short act of worship, a hymn sung unaccompanied and a brief address. It was a test to see how I would cope taking a service under different circumstances. The course officer was a delightful man named Roy Harding and our paths were to cross a number of years later when he and his family were regular worshippers at St Anne's, the dockyard church in Portsmouth. Roy was the commander of *HMS Intrepid*.

We went up the Dart and completed the waterborne exercise. Then we were dropped off from the boat and had to make our way across country to rejoin the boat by a given time and location. We speed marched through villages and the countryside until we were down on the shingle beach. We had been warned that if we were not back in time the boat would sail without us. It concentrated the mind and motivated us. With one exception!

The 'one' was an international student from warmer climes and he really did not want to know. Someone suggested that we leave him behind, but that was not feasible so we had to 'support' him. It really slowed us down. By now it was dark and as we ran, slipping and sliding across the pebbled shore, I ran into a rock which was about three feet high and went crashing over it, landing on my back, winded. We did make the boat on time, but when I went into my pocket, I found that my glasses case was badly dented and my glasses broken. It meant that my remaining time in Dartmouth was rather blurred and it taught me the value of a spare pair of glasses!

A respirator drill proved very painful. We were given a briefing about chemical smoke (CS) and then taken into a room where a pellet of CS was ignited and the compartment has a thin haze. We then had to take off our respirators say 'Gas, gas, gas' and exit via the door. The problem was that I opened my eyes because I couldn't remember where the door was. I suffered instant blindness; fortunately, my companions leapt forward and dragged me out into the fresh air, but it took a while for my eyes to clear. It was like peeling a ton of onions in one go. It was a mistake I never made again.

My glasses might have come in useful too when it came to parade training – in other words marching – but I doubt it. I did not excel at it and during one circuit of the parade ground I finished up with my chin against the wall because I couldn't figure out how to change direction 'left'. Everyone else went left, but I went straight on, much to the suppressed hilarity of the training staff and my fellow students. But the Colour Sergeant Royal Marines was not amused.

On leaving the parade ground I was summoned once again to the staff office and informed by Roy Harding that the course that I was on was only scheduled for two weeks as the others were predominantly Reservists so there was little point in remaining as they couldn't run a course for one and there was no other course that I could transfer to, so I was to be returned to unit (RTU). Why I wasn't told that at the very beginning I do not know but the parade training was the culmination of two weeks which I will never forget and set me on the path to the future.

I returned to Lympstone and my first call on Saturday morning was to the opticians in Exmouth. The next day a surprise awaited me because after church Ray told me that as my course at Dartmouth had finished early, he had arranged for me to get some 'sea time'. His friend was the captain of *HMS Bristol* and he had agreed to take me with them for two weeks' sea time to Norway. The following day, having repacked my kit overnight, I caught the train to Portsmouth to join *HMS Bristol*.

Chapter Two

Sea Time in HMS Bristol

HMS Bristol was a one off. She was built as one of eight escort vessels for the CVA (Carrier Vessel Attack) 01 carrier which was going to be named Queen Elizabeth, and she was intended to replace *Ark Royal*, but the Labour Government cancelled the orders and *Bristol* became a hybrid. She was a large ship, classed as a destroyer but much bigger than the Second World War destroyers. Her role became 'weapons trial ship' which meant that on Monday mornings she sailed from Portsmouth to Aberporth on the west Wales coast where there is a Ministry of Defence (MOD) live firing range, to conduct various test and trials of weapons. Then on Friday she would sail back to Pompey. It was a steady if boring routine, except that one Friday, during her return journey to Portsmouth, a fire broke out below decks. Fire at sea is greatly feared by sailors and there is a set procedure to follow.

On discovering a fire, the person closes the door from the outside and then telephones the officer of the watch on the bridge. The person then shouts 'fire, fire, fire' and gives the location of the fire and waits until the firefighting party arrives. On the occasion in question, the location was not given and the caller toddled off to his mess deck to have a cup of tea. By the time the fire was located, it had a strong hold and a little bit of panic set in. The wrong bore hoses were coupled up and the result was that the amount of water in the compartment was too great and caused the ship to 'loll'. This is when the water sloshes from side to side following the motion of the ship and causes it to move from side to side with increasing motion. It can cause a ship to capsize. Fortunately, *Bristol* was not far from Milford Haven and two tugs rushed to her aid. They straddled the ship to prevent the motion getting worse and the fire was eventually extinguished.

The damage was great. Two of her four engines were out of action and when I joined many weeks later, the bulkheads aft my cabin were buckled. She was due to go into deep refit on our return from Norway. I was thrilled to be on board and gratified to receive the greatest of welcomes. I had no experience of life on board ship and boy, did I make mistakes aplenty! I put my foot in it at every turn, but everyone was so kind and helpful. It was a wonderful training period for me because when I did go to sea properly, I was fully aware of all the 'dos and don'ts' but still managed to get it wrong from time to time.

Our destination was the port of Stavanger. This was my first run ashore, and on reflection, it was incredibly boring. (For the layman I should explain that 'a run ashore' is a term used to describe a night out on land.) It was a long time ago and things might have changed, but at that time Stavanger was a rather boring place. Its main claim to fame was the fact that they were building oil rigs there, but there was precious little else to commend it as a run ashore. The buildings were pretty and colourful, but the only pub in town was in the railway station and it was very expensive.

On the Thursday evening we hosted the traditional cocktail party which was the standard routine for a visiting ship. It was a time to provide hospitality and entertainment for local dignitaries and ex-pats, local businesses and perhaps diplomats. It's an opportunity for people to come on board and be given a tangible 'thank you' for what they've done in the past or for what they going to do in the future. Many businesses or organizations ashore help to make a sailor's life that little bit better. At the party, I witnessed the extraordinary sight of a lady dressed in a beautiful gold lamé dress roll a cigarette. She took a tobacco pouch from a little handbag and in John Wayne fashion, rolled a cigarette one-handed. I asked her if she would like one of mine which was Benson and Hedges and you'd swear I'd offered her a bar of gold because she exclaimed, 'Oh my goodness, Benson and Hedges! They are so expensive here.'

On the Saturday afternoon, there was another first for me – a 'banyan'. It's a kind of nautical picnic. We were able to use the captain's motor launch and went off to one of the islands in the fjord and had a picnic which was all very pleasant and great fun. On the Saturday night when we got back for supper, I heard that a John Wayne movie was on and everybody decided to stay in and watch it. The television lounge in *HMS Bristol* was formerly a radio compartment above the wardroom, but in a previous refit, because of Bristol's unique status, dockyard mateys were persuaded, perhaps with duty-free cigarettes, to incorporate the radio compartment into the wardroom itself. A spiral staircase was duly incorporated that led up to the newly created television lounge. It was all terribly grand. Anyway, on the Saturday night we settled down to watch the television and there was a sort of Norwegian

'Jim'll Fix It' programme, followed on prime-time television, not by John Wayne but by the 'Private Life of the Cuckoo'. I think that said it all. Sadly, I was blamed for the failure of Norwegian television to produce a cowboy film. The only moment of real entertainment on the trip was when we arranged a football match against the local Norwegians, although they didn't seem too interested.

There was a wider and more significant background to all this. At the time, Britain was in dispute with Iceland over fishing grounds and the so-called 'Cod War' was taking place. It was in its final throes, but the Norwegians tended to view Icelanders as their younger brothers, so they were not pleased with our presence. The captain discussed the situation with the heads of department, and then announced: 'Okay, enough of this. Let's go home.'

We 'pulled up the pick' and headed back to Portsmouth forty-eight hours early. On the way home, I conducted services on the Sunday, Holy Communion in the morning and Evening Prayer in the late afternoon, it being Whit Sunday.

I was also able to conduct a 'burial' at sea for the first time. Ray had encouraged me to visit mess decks and departments. During one mess deck visit one of the sailors asked if I did burials and I said that I did. 'Great' he said, 'can you bury our messmate?' 'Your messmate', says I (I had not heard of anyone dying on board!), 'Yes' he said and went behind a curtain and produced a brick! A common building brick.

He then explained that during the previous year, whilst on a run ashore in Portsmouth, he and his 'oppo' returning to the ship picked op this brick and started throwing it back and forth between them. A passing Petty

Officer, also from Bristol saw them messing about and 'tore them off a strip' and added, 'If you love the bloody brick so much you can take it back on board and I will check'. He did.

With typical naval humour it was then decided to enter the brick onto the ship's book and the brick was rated s Able Bodied. So AB Brick became part of the ship's company. So with painful looks they pleaded their case, 'See, Bish (that the sailor's affectionate name for chaplains) when we get back to Pompey we are paying off and the ship will be empty. We can't bear to think of our pal lying on some pile of building stuff. So we would like to give him a proper exit from the Service like'.

I thought they were taking the 'mickey' out of me at first so I said, 'You get permission to do this and I will bury him'. I thought it was a hilarious idea and approached the captain warily because being a 'makee learnee chaplain' it would be easy to get something else wrong and appear a complete prat. The captain, of course, knew all about AB Brick and readily agreed.

So it was that on our return passage that the engines were stopped and the committal took place. It was properly done with a piping party, a boats Ensign covering the body and I was properly attired in cassock and surplice. The words of part of the burial service were said and AB Brick slid to his eternal rest at the bottom of the North Sea. It was a great example of the humour that was common to the navy that I was growing to love.

Once back home, I was able to have a run ashore in Portsmouth for the first but by no means the last time. It was a place that I was to come to know very well over the years, but at that time it was still new to me. The following morning, I caught the train back to Lympstone.

My weekly routines were unchanged, but my preparation for the commando course in September began with a physical assessment test at the gym conducted by a physical training instructor. It was gruelling to say the least and it exposed the fact that I was totally unfit. After an hour (it seemed like days!) I arrived back at my office with a pain in my chest and every muscle twitching and aching. It was most unpleasant. I was thirty-one years of age and I had never run a mile in my life. I was looking at all these very fit people charging around with great gusto and enthusiasm and it was disconcerting. I'm afraid my heart began to quake because one of the reasons I had been sent there was to do the commando course as a prelude to joining 40 Commando.

My mind was distracted from my physical shortcomings when a few days later Ray said he needed to prepare me for the forthcoming Chaplain's Conference at Amport House, the Royal Navy and RAF Chaplains' School. Amport House had been a private manor house but was commandeered during the war and remained in the hands of the MOD. Not knowing what to do with it, the MOD eventually handed it over to the chaplains' branch of the two services. The army had its own school at Bagshot Park.

Amport is a small village near Andover and a delight, so attending the conferences was always a great pleasure. But this was my first one and I was very apprehensive at meeting so many of my fellow chaplains all at once. The week was very organised with the usual chapel services each day and speakers on a variety of subjects. In the evening we would stroll down to the village and sample the fare at the Black Swan public house, aka 'The Mucky Duck'. It was such a pleasure meeting the likes of Jack

Burgoyne, Arthur Nunnerly, Martin Orme and others who were coming to the end of their service, while at the same time meeting and making friends with others.

On Thursday we had a mess dinner when the guest speaker was the Second Sea Lord, and another guest was Lord Louis Mountbatten to whom I was introduced. He struck me as a very arrogant man and spoke in a drawl. He enjoyed being the centre of attention and regaled us – me in particular – as to how his first command, *HMS Wishart*, was the only ship mentioned in the Lord's Prayer, 'Our Father wish art in heaven'. People chortled at his 'wit', but I thought it extremely blasphemous. I met Mountbatten on another occasion and he repeated the remark.

The dinner was a completely new experience for me but one that I quickly got used to. One of our number, Reg Sweet, had forgotten his mess uniform and had no transport, so I took him down to Portsmouth to collect it from his ship *Intrepid*. This paid dividends for me because I travelled independently from Ray Roberts and, on completion of the conference, I was able to drive back to *HMS Bristol* in Portsmouth to collect a case of wine. As I mentioned earlier, *Bristol* was going in for a refit and the wine cellar was being sold off. I had bought a case of Nuit St George, so I called in to collect it and then made my way back to Devon.

On my way through Dorset, I was going down a hill with a village at the bottom when a policeman stepped out from behind parked cars and held up a hand signalling for me to stop.

I was in clerical collar and when I came to a standstill, the officer said to me, 'Padre, your speedometer runneth over.'

I said, 'Yes, I'm very sorry.'

'Where are you going?'

'I'm on my way to Devon. I serve in the navy.'

'I was in the navy myself.' He chuckled, and added, 'Mind how you go and don't go too fast in future.'

I didn't think I was going that fast, but I wasn't going to argue with him.

The weekly routines at Lympstone followed a similar pattern. On Sunday there were two services, an 0800 celebration of Holy Communion and a later service which was a sort of chopped about Matins, followed by a shorter version of Holy Communion. They weren't usually well attended, though the Commandant, Colonel David, and Mrs Bailey would be there, and perhaps the duty officer and one or two others. The congregations were never great. My wife and children were there, although the kids often went to the church hall next door for Sunday School along with other youngsters.

Once a month, or when there had been a burst in recruitment, there would be a 'recruit troops Sunday' at which the latest recruit squad would be expected to attend church. It was never a long service and one of the recruits would read the lesson. The majority of them had never been to church before and some resented it very much, but they came anyway. We used to tell them to take the order of service with them and 'scribble a line on the back for your mums' and just write: 'Dear Mum, guess what, went to church this Sunday; what a turn up for the books!' It was the only occasion during their time at Lympstone that they would be expected to attend church.

On one occasion we had a young marine who vehemently objected to going to church. I went to see him and said: 'Look, if they asked you to do something difficult you would do it. So why not this?'

He told me, 'I don't believe in God.'

I said: 'That applies to half the bishops in the Church of England, but why make life difficult for yourself? This is expected of you, and the training staff will make your life difficult if you don't. I will come and sit alongside you and you don't have to sing the hymns; you don't have to say the prayers, but just be there for your own sake.'

He came along and I sat beside him, and although the corporal and sergeant of the troop glowered at him, he acquitted himself very well.

Another one of our tasks in the working week was to give recruits a lecture on the role of the chaplain in the navy. We emphasised that chaplains were there to help the men, whether they were Christians or unbelievers.

During the summer heatwave of 1976 training began early at around 0700 because people were passing out and fainting due to dehydration if they trained later in the morning. Running in full fighting order in the lanes around Lympstone is difficult at the best of times; that summer it was awful due to the high hedges which would channel the heat and cut out cooling breezes. The squads often came in for their lecture straight after a training run, so we would have a huge vat of orange squash ready which they would consume quickly to rehydrate themselves. We tried to make the lectures very informal and hopefully they took away the memory that the chaplains were kind enough to give them a drink when they needed it.

There was a mess dinner planned for leavers on the Thursday of the following week. It was to be my first without Ray's presence, so I would have to do both graces. The first is always Nelson's Grace and the second is usually more informal. Over the years, I have built up quite a collection of graces, but at that time I was very new and very nervous. It was such a glorious setting: drinks on the terrace beforehand with the sun going down behind the picturesque view of the River Exe. The officers wore scarlet mess jackets with gold braid and the band of the Royal Marines performed the Beating the Retreat ceremony. It was almost overwhelming and I wondered what my father would have made of it all. I've always been sad that I was never able to share the numerous mess dinners with him.

No matter what I did that summer, my thoughts repeatedly returned to my preparation for the commando course which I was due to take in September when I returned from leave. What I couldn't understand was that after arriving straight from a sedentary way of life, and having had a preliminary test which showed how unfit I was, why I wasn't placed in the hands of an instructor and gradually brought up to the level of fitness required. I was at least ten years older than the recruits, but it didn't happen and I had to try to get myself fit. My efforts failed to pay dividends.

In September I reported to the training office and the whole debacle of my attempt to win the 'Green Beret' began. I eventually completed ten of the twelve 'Green Beret' tests and it was not an enjoyable experience. I was unlikely to decide to go back and do it again. For the uninitiated, the commando course lasts something like six weeks but not for those who wished to become marines. Their training went on for twenty-six weeks, while people like doctors, dentists and 'schoolies' (instructor officers) and me, had a scaled-down course. You were deemed to be professionally qualified, but the aim was to get you to reach a high level of fitness, so you could work alongside the Royal Marines.

There was a five-week preparation called 'The Beat Up' to get you into a prepared state and then the six-week course itself. It comprised very physical activities that challenged the human body. At thirty-one years of age, having never run a mile in my life, I was pitchforked into a maelstrom of activity. The so-called Tarzan Course was the main problem because I did not have much of a head for heights. The course consisted of obstacles over ground and rope work which I did not enjoy and I fell off a few times. Self-preservation took over and I clung on for grim death and failed that test.

There were several chaplains' positional moves relying on me passing the 'Green Beret' and being appointed to 40 Commando, Royal Marines. The fact that I failed the course did not disturb the plan at all. The Chaplain of the Fleet and the Commandant General agreed that I would be accepted with a blue beret, providing I had done all the other commando tests. I therefore joined 40 Commando in January 1977.

One lasting memory of Lympstone was of an incident at Christmas that year. An invitation had been extended to the warrant officers and sergeants' mess to come to the officers' mess for drinks and a buffet supper. This had been a custom for some time and the venues alternated. Ray and I had a prior clergy engagement, but we called in at the start and then left for our next engagement.

After lunch the following afternoon Ray was incandescent with rage. He stormed off to the colonel to complain that in a world where children were starving to death, the fact that grown men had spent more than £1,000 on booze the previous evening was a disgrace.

One of the dentists, who had his own tray of gin and tonics and went from group to group, had wandered home that night and collapsed in a hedge. His wife found him at 0200 and the frost had begun to descend. He could have died of exposure. It was not what Christmas was supposed to be about.

Chapter Three

40 Commando, Royal Marines

On 10 January, 1977, I was officially appointed chaplain to 40 Commando Royal Marines. It snowed heavily the night before I was due to start, so my journey from Lympstone was delayed. The motorway and side roads were closed and I joined up twenty-four hours later.

I had a very good handover thanks to the outgoing chaplain, Christopher Jarman, known as 'Kit'. He had been a naval chaplain for some time and had been with 40 Commando before, including two tours of Northern Ireland. In fact, they had almost been back-to-back tours. Now came a period of 'rest', so people could go on courses, move on to other units and get to know their families once again.

During my time with the Commando nothing like Northern Ireland took place, but it was never dull. 40 Commando was commanded by Lt Col Julian Thompson who later gained fame in the Falklands Conflict. The unit was based at Seaton Barracks in Crownhill, Plymouth. Previously based in Singapore, it had been brought back by the government under the east of Suez policy. A teak elephant, a memento of its time in the Far East, resided in the entrance hall of the officers' mess and berets were placed on it when entering the hall.

Seaton Barracks belonged to the army and was rented by the Royal Navy. A dual carriageway passed through Crownhill. On one side was Crownhill Fort, which was occupied by 59 Commando Engineers, an army unit; 40 Commando were on the other side of the dual carriageway and the relationship between 59 and 40 was always sensitive. In my role as chaplain, I endeavoured to share my time between both units. That is not to say that my time with the Commando was uneventful, far from it. Within three days of my taking over, a murder took place in Seaton Barracks.

One Friday night, two marines had gone into Plymouth and during the course of the evening one of the marines had met a girl. The couple left the other marine and came back to barracks. They climbed into bed and were found there by the remaining marine. He was the worse for wear from drink and a shouting match ensued. The first marine jumped out of bed to pacify him, but the other marine pulled out a knife and stabbed his friend. The girl was a nurse and she tried to help, but the victim was already dead. The guard was called, as were the police, and the attacker arrested. He was eventually taken to Exeter prison where I went to see him. He showed no sign of remorse; not then or on any subsequent visit. I believe he was found guilty and served a life sentence.

A more pleasant visit was a trip to meet the Bishop of Plymouth. Naval chaplains are encouraged to be part of the local clergy chapter and as such we should visit the local bishops and introduce ourselves. We must never forget that we are part of the wider priestly ministry of the church.

At this time, I moved my family down from Lympstone to 13 Charlton Crescent, Crownhill. This was one of a number of houses which were officers' married quarters. Further down the road there was a very large married quarters estate where the families of marines, sailors and soldiers occupied houses.

On 17 February, the funeral service of the dead marine took place in his home town of Warrington. His family invited members of his troop, the troop officer and me to attend. To do this we had to arrange an exercise with the Royal Marine Reserve, Liverpool, because the marine was not entitled to a full military funeral. We were billeted at *HMS Eaglet,* the Royal Navy Reserve and Royal Marine Reserve establishment in Liverpool.

I conducted the funeral during which military honours were paid. The family were very grateful for our presence and offered us great hospitality and kindness; so much so, that we missed the train connection. We caught the next train, but there were no further connections for our onward journey. As a result, when we arrived in Bristol Temple Meads Station at 2200, most restaurants, pubs and cafes were either closed or closing. It was a very cold night. We had a choice: we could either stand on the station platform and freeze while waiting for the train which was not due until 0100, or find somewhere warm to wait. We did the latter and ended up in a strip club of a less than salubrious variety. At least we were able to get a drink. The entertainment was awful, but nobody died of hypothermia.

At the appropriate time we left the club, retrieved our kit from the lockers at the station, and caught the train. We arrived in Plymouth at around 0400. I was summoned the following morning to the colonel's office. The colonel said: 'Can you explain why you and your party ended up in a strip club last night?'

I discovered that the troop officer had laid the blame at my door! I quickly pointed out that I had just conducted the funeral of a dead marine and had no desire to conduct another funeral because someone had frozen to death. The colonel accepted my reasoning and the story quickly circulated round the rest of the unit. Most of the personnel agreed with my argument and actually thought it a great hoot.

Life continued with the usual round of visiting hospitals, sick bays and married quarters, getting to know the people of 40 Commando and 59 Engineers. During the course of a conversation with Major Geoff Field, the officer commanding 59 Engineers, he told me that the unit was off to Cyprus for a month. It had been tasked with renovating the roads to the live firing ranges at Akamas on the west of the island. Bridges, culverts and the road surface needed to be repaired and the work was to take place from 13 April until 12 May. He invited me to join them, subject to Colonel Julian's approval. When I asked the colonel, he told me the Commando were not doing anything except a small exercise in Scotland over a long weekend, so by all means I could go with 59 and get to know them. I think he was happy that I wouldn't be on the weekend exercise in Scotland. Either way, I was happy to accept Geoff Fields' offer and looked forward to it. The Chaplain of the Fleet, now Basil O'Ferrall, was not impressed. He felt that I should be with 40 in Scotland but could understand the need to get to know 59.

On 13 April, I travelled to Brize Norton with 59 Engineers for a flight to Cyprus on board an RAF VC 10 aircraft. Our original flight was due to leave in the afternoon, but we didn't fly until 0050. We arrived in Cyprus at 0550 and moved into our accommodation at the sovereign base area. I was billeted with a Royal Marine major called Robin Lumley-Harvet. He was the officer commanding the medical squadron and became a constant companion, a great support and very good company.

We had a security briefing from the OC, Major Field, and then settled into our surroundings. We were welcomed by all and sundry and after a six-mile speed march we were entertained to drinks in the nursing sisters' mess. We were to be in Cyprus for two weeks and the fortnight was filled with the usual activities such as exercises, church services, entertainment and work.

Half the unit went down to Akamas and began work on the roads and the other half were involved in things like personal weapons training and other military activities. I was assigned a Land Rover and travelled between the two halves of the unit, accompanied by Robin who doubled up as churchwarden and driver. I took part in weapons firing including a Carl Gustav anti-tank rocket and throwing live grenades, it's the only time that I've ever thrown grenades and I have to say I was very apprehensive.

One afternoon we drove to a beach where there was a beach hut bar. It was closed, so we went off for a swim in the chilly Mediterranean. By the time we came out of the water, which wasn't long, the bar had opened and beer, nuts and crisps had all been laid out for us. The Greek Cypriots are nothing if not industrious and hospitable.

The following evening, I was invited to supper by Jack, a major in the Education Corps. I arrived at his house and his wife, a diminutive lady, opened the door. The reason Jack had asked me for supper was because we shared the same surname. I had never been that interested in genealogy, but he was, and he showed me a parchment that he and his wife had compiled. It traced the family name back to its origins in Normandy. It was a fascinating story and opened my eyes to the history of my family.

Apparently, it all began with a minor nobleman whose name was Tankred Guichard d'Hautville he was the lord of the manor which contained the town of Hautville sur Mare. He had eleven sons who were all warriors. The eldest, William, went south to Italy to make his fortune and became quite a powerful man. Some of his brothers followed and one, Robert, became one of the most feared and powerful men in southern Europe. He was a leader of the first Crusade. He conquered Sicily and established his brother on the throne of Sicily. It seems that at least one of the brothers came across with the Conquerer and eventually fought in the lowlands of Scotland. The Normans were, after all, mostly mercenaries. Anyway, it seems that he stayed in the area and the name went through one corruption from Guichard to Wishart. I was amazed to find out that there is a Wishart House in Portsmouth opposite the cathedral. If I could afford it, I would buy it. There was also a ship named after my family.

It is important that when service personnel are away they keep in touch with their families. The day after dining with Jack Wishart and his wife was Mary's birthday day, so I phoned home to speak to her and catch up on all the news with my wife. I then spent the rest of an invaluable day with the soldiers on the electric firing ranges. Targets race along electric rails and you shoot at them as they move. It is quite a challenge and it enabled me to get alongside the soldiers in their own environment. I was able to chat to them during the long periods between shooting.

I was doing very well in getting to know the soldiers, so on Sundays we had reasonable congregations. The best was on a Sunday evening when we had travelled down to Akamas, only to find that the RAF Regiment had put up their tents on the intended outdoor site of my church. With mock indignation, I confronted the flight lieutenant in charge and demanded that he moved his tents. He refused but suggested another site and offered to come to church by way of penance.

I celebrated Holy Communion on the beach and not only the flight lieutenant turned up, but there were a good number of others who came to church too. Following the service, we adjourned to the main mess tent where lively discussions took place late into the evening. I discovered, not for the first time, that there is an interest in the Christian faith by young men who do not usually come to church. Chaplaincy in all its forms is at the cutting-edge of evangelism.

The following morning Robin and I drove to the Troodos Mountains rest camp where we spent a few days. During this time, one beautiful morning, when the sun was shining and it was quite warm, we went for a walk. As we went along the road, in flip flops, shorts and T-shirts, we were stopped by Greek soldiers who levelled their weapons at us and demanded we go back. We had inadvertently strayed into a high security area which contained an early warning system. Fortunately, we had our ID cards and we sheepishly apologized and turned around. Not many minutes later the sky went black and it began to snow heavily. By the time we got back to camp, we were frozen, much to the amusement of the guard. A few brandy sours in the 'Pig and Whistle', the camp 'pub', soon warmed us up.

We returned from the Troodos rest camp to Dhekelia, in the south-east of the island, and then moved on to Akamas where I took evening service on a volleyball court. The following day we visited troops working on the road and the bridges, and helped drive some of the vehicles. We then stayed in Episkopi and had time to visit a number of ancient sites before returning home in mid-May having enjoyed a memorable trip.

I arrived back in 40 Commando just in time to go to the training camp at Lydd and Hythe in Kent. It was a large MOD site which incorporated a number of facilities. It's on the coast and well away from any built-up areas. There are live firing ranges and a mini village which is used for training in urban warfare and crowd control. When the 'troubles' in Northern Ireland were ongoing, all units that served there had to pass through Lydd and Hythe and train in riot control.

The reason we went there was for personal weapons training: five days of shooting. The panniers were packed and loaded onto lorries and the troops were to travel by coach. Some left early as an advance party including my friend, Ian Riddle, the doctor.

The day before we were due to leave, I had a phone call from the doctor telling me he had failed to pack his personal weapon, a 9mm Browning pistol, in the medical panniers.

He explained, 'It's still in the armoury. Do you think you can help Michael?'

Could I help? It was an awkward one. Quite why he phoned me I have no idea, but I wandered over to the armoury and asked the corporal, who was not going to Lydd, if he would release the weapon for the doctor. The corporal asked me to sign for it and it was delivered into my care. I placed it under lock and key in my office and collected it the next morning prior to getting on the coach. We were travelling in uniform, that is, denims and camouflage jackets. Since my panniers had already gone I slipped the pistol into the pocket of my combat jacket and boarded the coach. We stopped at Gordano service on the M5 near Bristol for breakfast and again in another service area on the run down to Kent. I have often mused that no one knew I had the pistol on my person. It was empty, but that's not the point. I could have got into a heap of trouble had it been known. When we got to Lydd I went to the armoury and handed the weapon in. The doctor owed me one.

I did not have a personal weapon but was able to draw one from the armoury. I proved adept with the pistol and passed the range course first time. Purely out of interest, the colonel had four attempts before he passed. Our second in command, Major Sam Bembrose, thought I should be in the Corps pistol team, but I don't think the Chaplain of the Fleet would have approved.

In the evenings we relaxed in the historic surroundings of 'The Woolpack Inn' in Hythe. It was a traditional olde worlde English pub with wattle and daub walls, dark beams and a huge inglenook fireplace where four of us sat, two either side of the fire. The pub dated back to 1410 and had been a haunt for wool smugglers. It was a delightful place to unwind after the rigours of the training camp.

On 5 June, the Commando moved to London in preparation for the Queen's Silver Jubilee celebrations. We were billeted at Hounslow Barracks and on the Sunday morning the men who were acting as 'markers' along the route, had a rehearsal at 0600. It was teeming with rain, but I went with them on the coach. I had a very large bag of toffees in my pocket and I was in clerical suit, collar and raincoat. The marines told me that once they were in position they couldn't move, so I went up and down the lines asking if they'd like a toffee. If they did, they opened their mouths and I would pop a sweet in, a small gesture which brightened the morning.

Eventually, I took shelter in a shop doorway. A policeman joined me and asked who I was, and what I was doing. I suspect he thought I was some sort of weirdo who liked giving sweets to soldiers. He was suitably embarrassed when I showed him my ID card and asked if he'd like a toffee. He smiled and said, 'Yes, please!'

On the day of the Jubilee, the Commando was mounting guard along Fleet Street and Ludgate Hill and on up to St. Paul's Cathedral. The sick bay team, to which I had attached myself, was in a separate street and I was in naval uniform with clerical collar. There was a great festive atmosphere, so the doctor, Surgeon Lieutenant Ian Riddle, and I decided to join the festivities on completion of the parade. I then realised that a clerical collar would be a disadvantage and decided to wear a collar and tie. I was changing in the street, putting my shirt and stock into the back of the sick bay wagon, just as the Major General, London District was riding past on his great charger. Ian snapped to attention and saluted. The major general gazed down at me – a disrobing naval vicar – and I said hurriedly, 'Sorry sir, I cannot salute.' He gave me a broad grin and I returned a thin smile.

Ian and I then went off to The Ritz, thinking the people would buy us lots of drinks; in fact, there was nobody there because they were all outside Buckingham Palace. It cost a small fortune for two halves of beer. We felt very deflated as we caught the tube back to Hounslow Barracks, and had our legs pulled by all and sundry.

A week or so later I travelled to Swansea to see the new Bishop of Swansea and Brecon because we were encouraged to keep in touch with our former dioceses. The bishop was called Benjamin 'Binny' Vaughan. I did not know it at the time, but we were to become good friends. On that first occasion, we met in the Dragon Hotel and his lovely wife was present. They were both very kind and hospitable.

A few days later the last 'Spithead Review of the Fleet' took place. It's extremely unlikely that there will ever be another one because the Royal Navy is now a shadow of what it was. *HMS Bristol*, in which I had served briefly, was towed out at night because she had no engines, but their Lordships wanted as many vessels on show as possible.

The Royal Yacht steamed slowly up and down the lines of warships, including ships from other navies. As the Queen took the salute, each ship, in turn, gave three cheers to Her Majesty. It was a great spectacle. I was only able to watch it on television after the event, but I was very proud to be a part of the Royal Navy.

Chapter Four

In Which I Apologize to the Archbishop of Canterbury

On 16 July, the Commando embarked on Exercise Forest Adventure, a test of the unit's capability to conduct a fighting retreat. At the same time, we were to assess the unit's skills in casualty handling. Due to the level of 'casualties', it meant corporals might end up commanding the remnant of companies.

The Commando drove through Plymouth to *HMS Cambridge,* the gunnery range just outside Plymouth and we were picked up by the helicopters of *HMS Hermes.* We flew around the Lizard and disembarked on the north Devon coast.

To begin with it was a beautiful day, but by the afternoon the weather had changed. On the high Devon moors the temperature dropped dramatically and the wind increased substantially. As it was meant to be a fighting retreat, we were constantly on the move. Digging shell scrapes (a shallow trench) meant hands were cold and wet and we ended up with real casualties suffering from frostbite and trench hand. Ian Riddle, our medical officer, actually wrote a paper for the Lancet on these injuries. Fortunately, the exercise didn't last long and we returned to barracks.

On 25 July, the Chaplain's Conference took place at Greenwich rather than Amport. This was because it was a full conference with all the navy chaplains present except those away at sea. The conference included a Triennial Dinner which made it a very grand affair. Retired chaplains were also invited to attend. Sadly, it transpired that this was the last Triennial Dinner of the Chaplain's Branch of the Royal Navy.

The conference included the usual business meeting with a number of speakers and on the Wednesday evening the dinner took place. Approximately two hundred people sat down to dine in the splendour of The Painted Hall of the Royal Naval College, Greenwich. The hall contains one of the most spectacular baroque interiors in the whole of Europe. It was a scheme that took the historical painter James Thornhill nineteen years to finish. After completion of the project in 1726, he received a knighthood and his work became known as 'Britain's Sistine Chapel'. In this august setting, the guest of honour was the Most Reverend Dr Donald Coggan, the Archbishop of Canterbury, who was being hosted by the Basil O'Ferrall, Chaplain of the Fleet. There were an enormous number of dignitaries and chaplains of other services and other navies present. Sitting alongside me on the night was the chaplain of *HMAS Melbourne*, who was a delightful Australian.

When the meal and speeches were over most of the people present adjourned to the bar which was accessed by an underground tunnel. As we were sitting at the end of the hall nearest the tunnel, we had to stand while the dignitaries passed by and we then rushed to get to the bar. In our haste, we caught up with the Archbishop and the Chaplain of the Fleet.

The Chaplain of the Fleet turned to the archbishop and said: 'I wouldn't stand there Your Grace.'

Dr. Coggan replied, 'Oh? Why not?'

As we passed, I muttered, 'Cos, you'll get killed in the rush!'

I didn't think I had been overheard, but I had been and was duly summoned to apologise. I did so, appearing suitably chastened. If you have to speak to an archbishop there are better ways of doing it! Still, the brethren thought it highly amusing. A very lively evening ensued and I saw the Bishop of Jarrow escorted to bed as he was not in full control of his legs. He wasn't the only one. A number of people had left their shoes outside their rooms to be cleaned. In a burst of working-class indignation, Ray Roberts prised open the lift door and threw a number of pairs of shoes down the lift shaft. I have no idea of the repercussions of his actions, but it was all part of a very raucous night.

On 5 August, the Defence Minister Patrick Duffy visited the unit and that evening the chaplains and their wives had dinner with the Chaplain of Fleet at Stonehouse Barracks. We then went on leave until the end of August.

Leave was always spent in Swansea. It was an unwritten agreement that since we lived away from home, we would spend leave periods at home in Swansea seeing friends and family. It's a lovely town but is now somewhat down-at-heel due to a lack of investment. When the children were small it had everything we needed – parks, beaches, sporting venues. The only thing it lacked was a constant supply of sunshine. When the sun went in, the leisure centre was the place to go. It had 'flumes' (water chutes that ran outside the building), an artificial 'beach' (tiles the colour of sand) and a wave machine. It was, and still is, the most visited attraction in Wales and we often had to queue. The children loved it.

When the sun was out, our favourite beach was Caswell or Langland Bay. We would go there first thing in the morning because we could get a parking place and spend the whole day on the beach, leaving at around 1600. We left in time to get the children home, bathed, fed and a story read to them. My mother always babysat without a murmur so Jeannetta and I could visit friends in the evening. We were never very late because I didn't think it was fair to abuse my mother's love and hospitality. Having said that she often came with us to spend the day at the beach with the children who, by now, were very interesting and great fun to be with.

The friends we visited in Swansea were people we had known for many years and they occasionally came to see us in Plymouth. We enjoyed a drink and perhaps a meal and it was always a joy to see them. It was always nice to enjoy a change of scenery and have a break from the demands of the Royal Navy.

But all too quickly leave was over and it was a return to Plymouth and back to duty. On my first day back in my office I had to prepare for an exercise called Goose Fair which was taking place in September. It involved three weeks on Salisbury Plain. My 'winger' (batman) and I would go through the schedules to ensure that we had all the kit that we needed. Since we would be living under canvas, we had to check that we had all the right bedding and personal equipment. I was to share a tent with my friend Ian Riddle, the doctor.

Before the exercise took place all the normal weekly activities were still ongoing – visiting families, organising baptisms and conducting services. In addition, I had long been unhappy with the state of the chapel and decided to try to get the funds to renovate it. I had to make a good case to the Supply Officer Commando Forces for funding. I also needed the permission of the Chaplain of the Fleet and the commanding officer, Colonel Julian, all of whom were more than happy to agree. Eventually, with their backing, and having obtained the necessary funding, I began to look for suitable establishments to provide what I needed.

The altar in the chapel had been in the chapel in the barracks in Singapore when it was overrun by the Japanese in 1941. The Japanese, true to form, sought to humiliate and misuse not only Christians but their chapels and places of worship. The chapel in the barracks had become a carpenter's workshop and the altar was used as a carpenter's bench. That has a certain irony! When 40 Commando returned to the UK the altar came with them. It lacked length, so I had it extended slightly so that an appropriate altar frontal could be used. I had the frontal made by Dingles, a department store in Plymouth. The store also supplied the backdrop curtain which covered the entire wall.

In one corner, we had a very large display of dried autumn flowers which was designed by the colonel's wife Mrs Thompson. The chapel wasn't frequented by many on a Sunday, but I felt that the unit deserved a chapel that looked like a proper place of worship and prayer. On display in the chapel was the battle ensign of *HMS Diamond* which had taken part in the debacle of the Suez campaign.

In complete contrast, another activity that I got involved with was the creation of the pistol club. I have always had an interest in shooting, particularly pistols. The club only met once a week and I couldn't always get there, but I almost bought a Smith and Wesson .38 calibre pistol for fifty quid. Common sense eventually prevailed and I didn't buy it.

I was capable of using firearms and it gave me another opportunity, albeit unexpected, to get to know the marines in a relaxed environment. On Wednesday, 14 September, Exercise Goose Fair began and I was scheduled to travel in one of the coaches with everyone else. But two days before the start of the exercise, four members of the advance party, who were there to set up camp, were involved in a car accident. They were all in hospital, two in a critical condition. One was in hospital at RAF Wroughton on one side of Salisbury Plain and the other was in Southampton General Hospital on the other side of the plain. Instead of travelling in one of the coaches, I took my own car so that I could travel back and forth between the hospitals. Driving a red Volkswagen Beetle in a military area caused a great deal of comment.

I had been looking forward to taking part in the exercise but had to put all that to one side so I could concentrate on visiting the sergeant who was in Southampton and the corporal who had been taken to Wroughton. By the time I was able to visit them, their families had arrived; one from Dumfries and the other from Plymouth. Comforting and counselling the families was my priority. The sergeant in Southampton had chest injuries and his recovery was already under way, much to the relief of his wife, family and the unit.

The corporal at RAF Wroughton was not so fortunate. He had sustained a serious head injury and was struggling on a life support system. His family required the greater level of support; nevertheless, I continued to squeeze in visits to the sergeant and his family in Southampton. Because of the distances involved, our Regimental Sergeant Major Bill Flatt, a delightful man, asked me why I was driving the long way round on main roads when I could cut across the plain using the tank tracks. It would save a great deal of time and fuel, he said.

I took Bill up on his suggestion. Salisbury Plain is criss-crossed by armoured vehicle tracks and he produced a map showing them. I made a copy and the following morning went to Southampton using the map as my guide. It was rough going but nothing the car couldn't handle. I was just thinking, great, I'm making good progress, when I turned a corner and came face-to-face with an enormous Chieftain tank! I swear my car went into reverse gear by itself and shot backwards into a lay-by. The tank rumbled past with its commander gazing down in astonishment at this red Beetle in the middle of nowhere, driven by someone in naval beret.

The days rolled on and sadly the corporal at RAF Wroughton made no improvement. It became clear there was no prospect of recovery. Finally, the doctors recommended that his life support system be turned off. It was agreed that it should be done on a given day and time, and I was there together with the family liaison officer to support the devastated family. I said prayers with them and then the machine was switched off. The corporal passed away peacefully. The family were distraught but had been prepared for his final moments. They asked me whether I would conduct the funeral. A few days later, I travelled with family liaison officers to Dumfries in the south west of Scotland to conduct the service. It was a tragic event which nobody could have foreseen. Both families were grateful for our support and all that we had done on their behalf – it was the least we could do.

Meanwhile, Exercise Goose Fair continued. The living conditions in the tented camp were quite amazing. When we moved from Seaton Barracks to Salisbury Plain everything was taken with us including pieces of furniture, the mess silver, and even the letter racks from the officers' mess. Why the mess silver you may ask? We intended to have a full mess dinner with the teak elephant on display (see above). Everything was prepared according to plan. The tables were covered with crisp, white tablecloths and the mess silver and candelabras were laid out to plan. Everyone was in mess dress. I said both Graces and we all enjoyed a very pleasant evening. There weren't any runs ashore because most personnel didn't have private vehicles or civilian clothes with them. But I had my car with me, so I and a few friends were able to visit one of the pubs in the area from time to time. It meant I was unusually popular.

Living in a tent is not my idea of fun. It was uncomfortable and damp, but it was September and we were in middle of Salisbury Plain. Fortunately, the sleeping bags were excellent. Royal Marines are used to living in holes in the ground, so I suppose that in comparison to that, a sturdy tent and reliable sleeping bag provide a modicum of comfort.

We undertook a lot of valuable training, but the exercise duly came to an end and we returned to the barracks at Crownhill. I resumed my normal duties which encompassed baptisms. These are always a great joy and a goodly number were done in my time at 40 Commando.

One that stands out was the child of CSM Pickles. Mr Pickles was the sergeant major of 59 Engineers and while we were in Cyprus his wife had given birth. Over a drink one balmy Cyprus evening, he had asked if I would be kind enough to conduct the ceremony at Seaton Barracks Chapel. I was delighted with the request. It had been for this very reason that the chapel had been renovated. The intention was that families could feel welcome and were surrounded by something that looked more like a chapel than a school room.

To undertake the baptism, I had to approach the Royal Army Chaplains Department because CSM Pickles was a soldier in the army not the navy. Our chapel was a naval one. The army were more than happy to grant me permission and the baptism took place one Sunday morning. Afterwards there was a reception in the sergeants' mess at Seaton Barracks. The baptism illustrated how barriers can be overcome by the simple expedient of a priest actually knocking on someone's door and saying, 'Hello, I'm …. How are you?'

I was glad that I was able to act as a bridge between the services and overcome some of the, I won't say hostility, but tensions that exist between the army and the marines. It was a delightful occasion and I was very happy and humbled that I was asked to conduct the ceremony.

On 26 October 1977, another life-changing event took place for me and my family. My son John was born at Freedom Fields Hospital in Plymouth at around 2200. His birth almost resulted in his mother's death as she hemorrhaged badly. Happily, she recovered and returned home after a few days. John was and remains a source of great joy for us and we gave him my father's name John Leslie. It's a name that is repeated down through the generations of my family. In the late 1970s there was none of the modern extended paternity leave that exist today. I had a few days leave while Jeannetta was recovering and then it was back to work.

There are always social occasions in any walk of life and the navy is no exception. These include when there's a change of command or simply someone leaving. On one such occasion, a troop run ashore was organised and four young officers got absolutely 'bladdered'. It was left to me to get them back to barracks. I propped them up against the wall by the taxi rank at Plymouth station and persuaded a taxi driver to take us back to Seaton Barracks. It was on the understanding that if any of them were ill and then sick I would have to clean it up. They weren't and we arrived at Seaton and I paid the taxi driver and thanked him for taking the risk. He helped me get them out of his taxi and I was able, one by one, to get them up the stairs and into their cabins. I sat them on their beds, took off their shoes, undid their ties, took off their jackets and put them in the recovery position. I spent the rest of the night going back and forth checking each one to make sure that they were sleeping peacefully. At breakfast the following day I looked dreadful; they looked as bright as buttons. They asked if I'd slept well and I said, 'No', but they didn't realise what I had done for them. Acts of kindness are the duty of a chaplain, in my opinion. If it were my son, I would hope that somebody would look out for him.

On another occasion, another troop run ashore at which an officer was marking his departure, there were people in a pub taking the 'mickey' out of the corps. The evening suddenly turned sour. It became tense and aggressive, and there was an outbreak of violence. A barman vaulted over the bar only for a marine to thump him back over the bar. Instantly, we were in the middle of a brawl. Two young troop officers wanted to get involved, but I grabbed them and bundled them out of the pub and into my car, before driving back to the barracks. They were cursing me, but I pointed out to that if they had got involved in the fight it could have ended their careers. If a marine is arrested for a punch up, he would get 'weighed off' (put on a charge) and lose his stripes, if he had any. He would also face a fine and stoppage of leave. Another possibility, for those young officers, would have been a court martial and the possibility of dismissal from the service. It wouldn't have looked too good on my record either. That incident was an example of good pastoral care.

Chapter Five

Green Goddesses – and the Season of Goodwill to all Men

In November 1977, Britain's fireman declared a national strike and the military was called in to protect the lives and property of the British public. There was a profound irony to this: the firemen were striking over pay and at the time soldiers, sailors and airmen were getting less pay than them. Whatever the rights and wrongs of the strike, we had a duty to do.

40 Commando Group had to take over a number of operational centres. Alpha company was stationed at Wolverhampton; 59 was at Coventry and other companies were preparing to move elsewhere in the country. At the next officers' O Group planning meeting, we were told the remainder of 40 Commando had to move to Glasgow, known as the 'tinderbox of Europe' because there were so many fires there.

The military was tasked with fighting fires and rescuing people with antiquated fire engines called 'Green Goddesses'. It was like something from an Ealing comedy film, armed forces servicemen racing to the assistance of the public with antique equipment. Green Goddesses had limited pumping and ladder facilities.

The police escorted us to fires or emergencies at which point we did the job of firefighters. I moved with the main body of men to Glasgow where we commandeered an empty block of flats on the western side of the city. The main headquarters was in the Territorial Army Centre at Maryhill. I was issued with a Land Rover, so I could travel between the locations, visiting the troops and trying to make myself useful by delivering mail. I offered to conduct services, but it wasn't practical to hold them because of the likelihood of us being called out. If the lads weren't on watch, they were in bed.

There was no time off. When leave was granted, it was called 'rest and relaxation' (RnR) and usually taken at home.

As Christmas approached and with no resolution to the strike on the horizon, it was clear that we would all be away from home for the festive season. The public thought this was very sad and people in Glasgow gave us vouchers, so we could go to one of the big department stores and buy food and condiments. Marines could either consume their little hamper in the 'barracks' or could take it home if they were going on RnR. I was detailed to serve on a 'committee of taste' along with a couple of officers. Our task was to find out what food was available and to make sure that everybody had a fair share. It was interesting because we went to one of the big department stores in Glasgow where we were greeted by the manager who gave us a tour of the shop and showed us what we could have and what we couldn't have. We then made our choices, had the products packed up and transported to our HQ at Maryhill. Once there, it was divided up into boxes with people's names on and distributed to the personnel concerned.

Thanks to the people of Glasgow, Christmas 1977 was truly one of goodwill to all men. I felt I had made a useful contribution in providing the troops with a little comfort at a time when they were missing their families.

Another thing I did was stand watches. We had to man telephones twenty-four hours a day because if there was an emergency the police would be in touch with us to get the nearest Green Goddess out. Volunteering to man the phones gave guys the chance to catch up on sleep or write to their families.

Of course, I was away from my own family too. By this time, we had three small children and I missed them greatly, but it was no good bleating about it. It was part of the job and sometimes in the military you have to be away. I often thought that phoning home on Christmas Day was a bad idea because it upset everybody.

That Christmas, because we were in the UK, telephone lines were made available to us for a limited time, so people could contact their loved-ones. I phoned home and found it very difficult speaking to small children and trying to explain to them why I wasn't there on Christmas Day. My wife tried to play down Christmas which is difficult when you've got young children. When I returned home on RnR, I had my Christmas, albeit a deflated one, but you had to make the best of it.

The Commando was operating in a number of locations including the West Midlands. One call in Coventry alerted the lads to an old lady's cat stuck up a tree. Mindful that this could be good PR, the marines diverted a Green Goddess on its way back from a 'shout' to rescue the errant 'moggie'. They found the location, got the ladders out and a marine went up, grabbed the cat and brought it safely down to earth. He handed it over to the relieved owner.

The old lady said, 'He's always doing this.' She thanked them and they got back into the Green Goddess, but as they drove away, the cat jumped out of the old lady's arms, ran under the back wheels of the vehicle and was run over and killed. There was no more tree-climbing for him.

The story made the national press. It spawned a flurry of jokes among the marines who are known for their unsentimental and robust sense of humour – a bit like mine.

The New Year dawned and we still found ourselves stationed in Glasgow. Our New Year's Eve and Hogmanay celebrations were rather muted because we were still on duty. It was interesting to be in Scotland at Hogmanay and witness how much more the Scots make of the New Year than they do of Christmas. I was amazed that some churches weren't open on Christmas Day, but they were on New Year's Day.

After nine weeks on strike, the firefighters eventually settled for a ten per cent pay increase, taking their average salary to just over £4,000. The Green Goddesses were put in to storage and regularly tested, so they could be used in the future during times of flooding or drought. They even made a comeback during the firefighters' dispute of 2002-03.

After two months away we were glad to return home. Not having seen the children for weeks it was good to see them and catch up on all they'd been doing and see what they had had from Santa Claus.

The marines were looking forward to their next trip overseas, a southern flank exercise mainly in Sardinia. But I had more pressing matters on my mind: we had to plan John's baptism. It was to take place on a Sunday in the chapel at Seaton Barracks. A number of people were invited, including Ray Roberts who was one of John's godfathers.

Two days before the event it snowed heavily, so instead of having thirty people at the baptism there were just half a dozen. The awful weather meant we couldn't get the car out of the garage and John was wheeled around to the barracks in his pram which, like us, was slipping and sliding everywhere. We couldn't postpone the baptism because all the food had been prepared. There was so much left over that I took it to the guard room to distribute to whoever wanted it. Marines are always hungry, so it didn't last long. As baptisms went it left much to be desired, but the main principle was that John was signed with the sign of the Cross.

It wasn't quite as hectic in early 1978 as it had been in previous years, but having said that the unit was designated 'Spearhead Battalion.' Spearhead Battalion is where one battalion of the British Army is placed on standby to go anywhere in the world at a moment's notice at the behest of the government. It might be to protect British people or British interests, or to quell a dangerous situation. The selected unit is on standby for a month. With 40 Commando taking on 'Spearhead' responsibilities, it meant lots of preparations being made and the panniers being packed for any eventuality.

I was driving out through the main gate one morning when the corporal of the guard stepped forward and held his hand up: 'I'm sorry sir, but you can't go out. We're on forty-eight hours' notice to move.'

I returned to my office and phoned my wife. I explained: 'We're not allowed to go out. Can you pack a few things for me and bring them to the back gate, so I can collect them?'

Everyone began to speculate as to where we were

going to be deployed. The consensus of opinion was that we were to be sent to Rhodesia. Only a few weeks earlier a bishop, a priest and two nuns had been dragged from a car and shot by terrorists operating within the country at the time. More than a decade earlier, in 1965, Ian Smith, the Prime Minister of Rhodesia, had announced a Unilateral Declaration of Independence (UDI). A guerrilla war had then started in 1975 in which Robert Mugabe hoped to unseat Smith and replace the predominantly white government with a one-party Marxist state. One rumour in circulation was that Spearhead Battalion would have to go in and confront troops of the Rhodesian Army.

It meant I was confronted with the classic moral dilemma for a chaplain: do I go armed or do I rely on other people to protect me? I didn't think it was fair to say to my batman: 'You go out and shoot those people while I stand here and pray.' I made the decision to contact someone I knew in Plymouth and ask them if they could provide me with a .38 Smith and Wesson revolver and ammunition, on a sale or return basis. If my plans had come to light it would have sent shock waves in all sorts of place and I would have been pilloried. But I stand by my guns, if you'll excuse the pun. I think it's wrong that if a chaplain is in a situation like that to expect other people to protect them. I had a wife, three small children, my mother and lots of people who cared for me and I wasn't prepared to stand there and play the martyr. In due course, a parcel appeared at the back gate and contained what I suspected. The revolver was safely tucked into my panier.

In the officers' mess that night there was a very informal meeting at which lots of people said they would not take up arms against the armed forces of Rhodesia. Feelings were running high. Some said they would rather resign their commissions. In the event our intended destination wasn't Rhodesia at all but Belize, and in the end we didn't go anyway. I returned the pistol, panic over. I was no longer faced with the moral dilemma of resorting to arms, but I reflected that if we had been deployed to a trouble spot my time in the pistol club would not have been wasted. Some people have asked me if I would be able to kill someone. The short answer is I don't know. That's the honest answer.

I was very conscious of the fact that as the children grew older, I was not likely to be around to help. At some stage my time in 40 Commando would come to an end and I would be moved elsewhere. It was likely that I would be sent to sea because I had originally requested a sea job. Serving with the Royal Marines is classed as a 'sea job' but I wanted the experience of ships. My time onboard *Bristol* had whetted my appetite. My wife and I talked about it and we felt the best place for the family to live was in Swansea where my mother and my mother-in-law and others could help Jeannetta with the children when I was away at sea. Not long after that discussion I was in Swansea on leave and went into the Abbey National and I asked if it was possible to have a mortgage.

The manager said to me: 'Do you have any money in your account?'

'I'm a member' I replied cautiously.

'Okay, let's have a look at your account.'

He looked at his screen and said: 'Oh! There's £6 in there, so yes you can have a mortgage'.

I was amazed. We began to search for a suitable house within the financial parameters laid down and eventually found one in the Landore area of Swansea. It was a three-bedroom terraced house, nothing exorbitant. With high hopes we went out to view it. There wasn't much of a garden but it served the purpose, so we bought it. It was preferable to living in married quarters in the south of England and meant a more stable home life for the children because my mother and my mother-in-law were always on hand to help. The girls went to the local primary school and made friends very quickly and they became part of the local church in Landore which had an excellent priest as vicar and an enthusiastic congregation. When I returned to Swansea on leave, I was regarded as a member of staff of the church and asked to preach and celebrate Holy Communion.

My usual pastoral activities continued, visiting hospitals and homes, baptising children and being available to anyone who needed me. The southern flank exercise in the Mediterranean now loomed large. It was to be a multinational force, troops from Italy, the USA, and the UK carrying out a number of serials to test the effectiveness of working together. We were to be away for a little over a month and the exercise was dubbed 'Dawn Patrol'. This was to take place on the island of Sardinia, so we embarked into the ships, *Sir Geraint* and *Sir Galahad,* both Royal Fleet Auxiliary supply vessels. We boarded them in the Hamoaze, a stretch of the River Tamar and in the shadow of the old *HMS Eagle*, which was awaiting disposal for scrap.

We arrived in Gibraltar on 8 May, 1978. That evening, a friend of mine, Hugh Affleck-Graves, C Company's commander, got himself into a bit of bother with a Gibraltarian policeman and I had to go to the police station to vouch for him. As soon as he was out of the police station, he carried on his merry way into bustling streets of Gibraltar. The next day we held a 'Top of the Rock' race as a bit of fun. Hugh was well ahead of me and threw small stones down at me, encouraging me to try to catch up with him. What gratitude! I never caught up with him. I think I finished something like 357th out of the entire Commando which wasn't bad. It was the first time that I had run 'The Rock', but you don't actually run to the very top because the summit is out of bounds. You run to the cable car station and that believe me is far enough.

We sailed for Sardinia the following afternoon. When we arrived at the assembly point there was an American assault ship already there and we set anchor nearby.

We needed to take currency onboard which the Americans had and I was asked to accompany the Imprest Officer over to the assault ship. The Imprest Officer is the chap who looks after the money within the Commando and since the troops would require foreign currency, he was the man to obtain it. We went over to the American vessel by helicopter, landed on the deck and went below. We were introduced to the American supply officer and he and our Imprest Officer went off to an office to count the money while I remained in the reception area. Two sailors were sitting behind the reception desk.

One of them asked me, 'Could you tell me where we are, sir?'

I fished a map out of my pocket and pointed out our location.

He said, 'Where is that?'

'The Mediterranean Sea – and that is the island of Sardinia where the exercise is taking place.'

'Thank you, sir,' he said. 'I thought that's where we were but wasn't sure.'

I was amazed that these men weren't certain of where they were. Perhaps they were pulling my leg, but it wouldn't have been the first time that I had discovered that Americans don't brief their people as well as they should.

After taking the money back to the ship we disembarked and set up camp in our allocated area on land. Crawling into my one-man tent that night, my right knee locked. I'd been having trouble with the knee for months. It would lock and be very painful, then suddenly unlock and be fine for some time until it locked again. There was little anyone could do until it reached a critical stage, and this appeared to be it. What a time to pick. I just couldn't straighten it and was in a great deal of pain. There was nothing I could do about it at that time of night except crawl into my sleeping bag and try to get some sleep.

I surfaced in the early hours of the morning vaguely aware of a thunderstorm going on and when I woke in the morning I was surrounded by puddles of water. I was dry since the Pusser's sleeping bag was very good in those conditions. My kit was dry too because I'd secured everything in plastic bags. But the tent, which was stamped 1955, was like a sieve. It hadn't been waterproofed in years and it was like sleeping in a shower.

Getting dressed while trying to straighten my knee was very painful, but I managed it and hobbled over to the Regimental Aid Post to see my friend Dr Ian Riddle.

I struggled into the medical tent and Ian, who was puffing on his pipe, said, 'Your cartilage has finally gone.'

'Yes, I need to go back to the ship'.

'Absolutely not,' he said.

'Why not?' I said. 'I can't do anything on this exercise.'

He said: 'If I've got to stay here, so do you'.

I reflected on the cruelty of people that I had chosen as friends and on the fact that there was nothing I could do about it; it would probably be far better for me to remain and have something to do, rather than lying on my bunk in a cabin with nothing to do and getting bored very quickly. It warranted an operation back in the naval hospital in Plymouth rather than in a tent in Sardinia.

I went to see the colonel and explained the situation and he said: 'Okay, we'll attach you to the heavy weapons platoon', which meant that I would be riding around in a Land Rover for most of the time. It was interesting for me because the heavy weapons platoon were the people who did fascinating things with explosives.

The exercise we were involved in was a multinational one – but with a twist thanks to the Italians. The British, Americans and Italians were meant to liaise with each other, but the Italians said they weren't prepared to play after Friday evening. On Friday afternoon their people all went home and the British and Americans carried on without them.

The Italians troops who took part in the exercise were mountain troops who sported wide-brimmed hats with great big feathers in them. They were very good soldiers when they turned their minds to it. Their ration packs were something to behold; the one we saw was a plastic bag and included a tot size bottle of cognac. Our ration packs were good and came in three varieties A, B or C with different foods in each one. As always, the Americans had more than everyone else. Our rations were in cardboard boxes which we would break up, so we could stow the items in our fighting orders. It meant we didn't have to lug cardboard boxes all over the place. The Americans on the other hand had cardboard boxes for every single meal. Their food was superb with menus like roast beef in gravy or roast pork and pineapple. It was amazing food and we were envious of them.

On one occasion we were scheduled to carry out a landing exercise using American craft because their landing ship was a lot bigger than ours and they had proper landing craft. It was to comprise C Company and the heavy weapons platoon in support. The Americans came and picked us up. I was hobbling at the rear, my leg permanently bent. I was put to work carrying the base plate for the 84mm mortar. We were transported to the designated bay but were not the most popular of interlopers. Although we were taking part in an official exercise, the Sardinians had made it plain that we were operating in areas of the island they did not want us to use.

Undeterred, our landing craft approached the beach and my friend Hugh Affleck-Graves had a bugler alongside him who was suitably camouflaged. The chap was a musician who had grown tired of performing in military bands and had become a marine. Hugh instructed him to blow 'The Charge' when the ramp went down and this he duly did. It impressed the watching 'brass' mightily. When he blew his bugle, a great shout went up from the troops and we charged ashore. I say 'charged', I couldn't charge anywhere. I sort of meandered forward as quickly as I could.

One marine asked: ' Sir, why can't we practise a Dunkirk?' I cannot repeat the reply his corporal gave him. Up the beach went the troops. The heavy weapons platoon, of which I was a proud but sluggish member, came down the ramp set up the 84mm mortar and dropped a Thunderflash into the barrel. There an enormous bang. Colonel Julian, who was there to observe how the proceedings went, almost shot out of his boots which was very funny but we were careful not to laugh.

The landing exercise continued until we arrived at our new base. Various activities were planned to demonstrate the skills of different elements of the unit: for example, the communications people displayed their electronic equipment and the heavy weapons guys their combat drills. We even had to simulate a nuclear explosion. It meant producing a mushroom cloud. To do that we had an oil drum filled with soap suds and other 'ingredients' and when it was full an explosive charge was attached to it. We hastily retreated and pressed the button. There was an almighty bang and it produced a mushroom cloud. I suppose in combat that could be quite useful as a decoy.

Another thing that I learnt with the heavy weapons platoon was how to use explosives if you wanted to blow up a tree to create a roadblock, or planned to cut a railway line, so people on the train couldn't see the damaged track. If the charge is placed correctly and in the right quantity the rail is cut as neatly as though a hacksaw has been used. Plastic explosives and chemical timers are quite amazing; just the kind of things that I would need to know when I returned to parish life! But it was good fun and I got to know the marines of the heavy weapons section very well indeed.

We returned to our bivouac area and lit a bonfire and ate our ration packs and enjoyed few cans of beer. I couldn't face the struggle of crawling into my tent with my bad leg and after checking with one of the sergeants I slept in the Land Rover. I had a wonderful sleep under the stars. It was a balmy evening and I was quite comfortable. Bearing in mind that we couldn't wash, shave or shower in the mornings, it didn't really matter where I slept. I woke the following morning fully refreshed.

When the exercise came to an end there was a stark difference between the way the Americans wrapped things up and the way we did – I'm sure it came down to financial considerations. The Americans and their equipment were air-lifted back to their ship by helicopters in about an hour. The British took a whole day because we had to embark on a huge raft called a Mexeflote which was really two huge rafts joined in the middle. It was an exercise in embarking vehicles from a beach situation. First, the heavy lorries were driven on, followed by the Land Rovers and personnel. Inevitably, there was a long tailback of traffic and while we were sitting on the sand watching the vehicles trundling onto the Mexeflote we spotted a fire further down the beach.

'Let's go and see what's going on,' I said to one of the medics.

When we arrived at the site of the fire, we couldn't believe our eyes. The Americans were burning their ration packs. They had not yet embarked their armoured vehicles and there was a top sergeant (a sort of CSM) who personified the typical image of an American soldier. He wore sunglasses, had a cigar clamped between his teeth and was shouting at his men: 'Come on you bastards. Get it right. You're making the place looks like Nancy's parking lot!'

I had no idea who Nancy was but went up to him and asked: 'Excuse me, Top, why are you burning the ration packs?'

'It would screw up bookkeeping, sir. It you want some, help yourself.'

We had been assigned to the Land Rover attached to the medical section and needed no second bidding. We grabbed armfuls of boxes of food and carried them back to our vehicle. Just ahead of us was the command vehicle, so I ambled along and asked the colonel if he would like some. (It pays to keep on the right side of superior officers.)

He said, 'Yes please', and we took a supply of rations to his Land Rover as well.

Word quickly spread and marines poured out of their vehicles to go and help themselves to the boxes of food. Better for it to be eaten than burnt. Having just settled back into the sick bay Land Rover, surrounded by this unexpected windfall, Hugh Affleck-Graves, the company commander of Charlie company, wandered over and said: 'Why don't you come back down to the beach with us?'

I left my kit with the sick bay team and went off with Hugh. We arrived at a section of the beach where his troops had glasses of red wine. He explained that he'd arranged with a local tavern to deliver some rough Sardinian wine to the beach, so they could have a drink before going back to the ship. It was a great idea that demonstrated true leadership qualities. Sometimes it's the small things that can keep morale up.

As the lads were chatting over their tipple, he whispered: 'For you and I, I have a slightly better bottle.'

We didn't have a bottle opener so I smashed the neck on the bonnet of the Land Rover. Fortunately, it broke neatly and we were able to enjoy a glass. I say 'glass', but to be accurate, we drank it out of Bakelite mugs. It was a fitting end to a two-week exercise. None of us had been able to have showers, and we were all feeling very dirty, so this small luxury was a delight. We were then loaded onto the Mexeflotes and headed back to the ship.

The ship then moved into the harbour. I think it might have been to refuel. That's where the remnant of 40 Commando rejoined us. I remember the colonel pulling up on the jetty and when he lifted his goggles there was a rim of dirt all the way around them, a legacy of operating in the more remote areas of Sardinia away from civilisation and the joys of a proper water supply.

I think that day was either Whitsunday or Trinity Sunday. I can't quite remember, but we did have services on board that evening. I was accompanied during this deployment by the Church of Scotland chaplain, Gordon Craig, a delightful man and a good companion. We shared a cabin and while on land he had done what I should have been doing, going around the whole 40 Commando force.

When *Sir Geraint* headed for home, the senior Royal Marine on board was Major Alan Hooper. Gordon Craig and I had a great working relationship with him. Gordon and I held joint services, a sort of hymn/prayer sandwich. I wore clerical robes, but being a Scottish Presbyterian, Gordon was dressed in 'stone' shirt and Lovat trousers. After we had had our service there would be a shortened Holy Communion and Gordon stayed to receive the sacrament. This did not mean that the Church of England was superior to the Scottish Presbyterian Church, he was merely boosting my confidence by adding another face to the congregation. We stopped off in Gibraltar and had a brief run ashore before heading home and arriving back in Britain in mid-May.

During the late summer there was a change of

command at 40 Commando. Lt Col Julian Thompson left the unit and our new commanding officer was Lt Col Martin Garrod, a brave and resourceful man who had already distinguished himself in a number of military operations. As a young subaltern serving in Borneo, he had led a squad of marines who had rescued British citizens taken hostage by terrorists. It had been a very delicate operation conducted at night and was a complete success. He had also been deployed to Northern Ireland where he was 'mentioned in dispatches'. Col Garrod went on to become Commandant General.

We then learned that the unit was to move to Northern Ireland on garrison duties at Ballykelly. It was a 'married accompanied billet' which meant I was expected to take my family with me. I was not too happy about this because they had just settled into the house in Swansea. I was reluctant to uproot them again and move them to Northern Ireland. Northern Ireland came under army control and it meant I would be operating under the Royal Army Chaplains' Department. I contacted them and outlined my dilemma. They were not at all sympathetic and there was a reluctance to even discuss the matter.

The next thing I knew, I had the Chaplain of the Fleet's office on the phone saying that if I wasn't prepared to move my family to Northern Ireland then I would have to move to another appointment earlier than planned. It wasn't going to be that early because I was due to be relieved from my post in Northern Ireland within a few months anyway. I just didn't see the point in uprooting my family for such a short time. I eventually left 40 Commando in December 1978. I had completed two full years with the unit.

Perhaps the most notable service that year was the

Remembrance Sunday service in November when the whole of Commando mustered and I preached the sermon and conducted the service. Colonel Garrod paid me the compliment of saying that it was the best Remembrance Sunday sermon he had heard.

I left 40 Commando towards the end of the month and was relieved by Andrew Rowe, a single man and a very experienced commando chaplain. Just before Christmas leave, I packed all my kit, loaded up the car and drove out of the officers' mess car park. I reached the main gate and handed in my car pass. The Corporal of the Guard said: 'Good luck, sir', and saluted. I drove down the dual carriageway towards Devonport ruminating on the stark realisation that another new phase of my life was about to begin. My intention in joining the Royal Navy had been to go down to the sea in ships. I was about to get my wish.

Chapter Six

For Those in Peril on the Sea

I arrived at the main gate of *HMS Drake*, showed my letter of appointment and drove in. I was issued with a car pass and there was the usual Royal Navy banter. It seems to me that the Navy has a greater rapport with its chaplains than the other services. At least it did then. Once I'd received my car pass, I drove down to the wardroom and parked my car. The steward at the wardroom reception allocated me a suite and a garage. I was surprised that I was deemed senior enough to warrant a suite: that is, a sitting room/study, a bedroom and a shared bathroom. I shared the bathroom with the commanding officer of a nuclear submarine who was rarely there, so effectively, it was mine.

I went down to the car, emptied it, unpacked, and then wandered around, familiarising myself with the layout of the mess. I had been in the building before but not as a resident. At supper the duty steward very solemnly informed me that my mess number was the traditional one for a chaplain, No 7, and he handed me a napkin and silver napkin ring. The following morning, I found out where *HMS Jupiter* was berthed. She was the leader of the squadron and as such 'HQ', so all my documents would have to be kept there until I needed them.

Arriving on board, my first task was to call on the captain, Geoffrey Dalton, a man I came to know very well. Then I met the officers who were available to have a chat at that time. Eventually, I handed my documents into the master-at-arms' office. I had no idea of the layout of the ship, but the master-at-arms found time to show me around. He introduced me to this person and that person, and it was all very informal and very informative, but the person that it was imperative for me to meet was the squadron operations officer. He was the man who had all the programmes for all the ships in the squadron and could smooth the way for my future duties.

We sat down over a coffee and cigarette and discussed what we were going to do. He explained: 'You can join ships at any time providing they have accommodation for you.' He showed me the programme and asked: 'Where would you like to start?'

I said: 'My objective would be to get round the squadron as quickly as possible, spending a short time in each ship, and then go back for a longer time on another date.'

He nodded 'That sounds a good strategy.'

I said: 'I don't care if they're in the Arctic Circle or the West Indies, or doing basic operational sea training or commanding officers sea training off Portland, but I would rather see them first time around under more difficult circumstances. Pitching up for a three-month tour of the West Indies is a cheek if you haven't been with them when the work is not so pleasant.'

'I entirely agree with you,' he said. 'Look, leave it with me for a day or two and I'll try and work out a rough programme for you.'

I was pleased at how well the meeting went but have

to admit that my tactful suggestion that I should visit ships under more difficult circumstances first was thanks to Ray Roberts who had given me that wise guidance.

Ray had also advised: 'Never go to a ship unless you have a cabin. It's not being over-demanding. You must have somewhere to say 'the Office' (a clergy term for Morning and Evening Prayer), to prepare your sermon, and see people who need to talk to you in private. After all, you *are* the squadron chaplain'.

The squadron operations officer sent signals to the other ships with the outline of a programme, and each ship responded with a message, either 'Yes, we can take the chaplain at that time' or 'No, we can't'.

The programme was adjusted as necessary, firmed up and each ship then received a programme confirming my movements. Once it was all approved, the captain having the final say, things like warrants were sorted out. I continued to meet people in various parts of the ship until the end of the working day and then returned to *Drake* wardroom and got ready for supper.

The wardroom was similar to the building at Dartmouth and the wardrooms at Portsmouth and Chatham, all very imperial and imposing. This one overlooked the main parade ground of the base. It boasted an excellent dining room with reliefs depicting the Armada on the upper walls. It was designed to seat about two hundred officers, but on that particular evening there were nowhere near that number eating. After supper, I adjourned to the bar, excused my non-uniform attire (commonly called 'rig') with the officer of the day, as per naval tradition, and had a drink with other 'inliers' who were all kind and friendly. A key characteristic of the navy is that people are quick to make one feel at home.

There were a couple of ships of the squadron in harbour at the time, so I visited them over the next couple of days and joined the other chaplains for daily services at St Nicholas' Church which served the barracks and naval base. After two days, I was able to set off for Christmas leave knowing that my programme had been finalised and agreed. It was with a great sense of excitement that I drove back along the M5 and M4 to Swansea, and it wasn't only because I was spending Christmas at home with my family.

That festive season was particularly special because it was our first one in the little house in Landore. We received a great welcome from the vicar, Reverend Arthur Howells, and the congregation of St Paul's Church. Arthur's wife Margaret ran the Sunday school and was great with the children. To my delight, I was invited to celebrate Holy Communion and preach at Midnight Mass. Without realising it, the seeds of returning to parish ministry were sown. It was a lovely service with a large congregation and as I sang the 'Prayer of Consecration' my voice came back to me off the walls – a moment which lives long in my memory.

We returned home in the early hours of the morning and put the children's presents under the Christmas tree. My mother had been babysitting for us and I drove her home. She was going to spend Christmas Day with us but couldn't stay overnight because we didn't have a spare bedroom. It was only a short ten-minute journey. Eventually, I got home and was relieved to place my head on the pillow after a long day.

At around 0200 I heard noises downstairs. Puzzled, I padded down the stairs to find that Sarah and Mary had opened every present including John's. There was wrapping paper from the front door to the back door. They were scolded for being silly and naughty children and put back to bed. Later that morning, the downside to their actions became apparent because they had no presents to open. They were very miffed and tearful when John was opening his presents (we had rewrapped them). A lesson has been learnt!

Christmas leave was a delight and all too soon I had to return to duty in Plymouth. The programme that I had worked out with the squadron operations officer, had me scheduled to join *HMS Antelope* in early January. Unfortunately, the snow intervened and I had to phone the ship to explain why I would not be there on time. Joining *Antelope* would enable me to get to know the routines of ship board life and provide a rough idea of the layout of ships.

Amazingly, I managed to get a line through to the ship via the dockyard exchange. Anyone who has tried that will know just how difficult it is, but I managed to speak to the first lieutenant and explained that because of the snow I couldn't travel. I reassured him that I would be along as early as possible the following day and he said not to worry that would be fine. I arrived in Plymouth midmorning and went to the ship immediately after lunch.

The ship was about to go into the maintenance sheds. At that time, the sheds were brand new constructions that enabled frigates to be worked on undercover around the clock. They were a brilliant design with interlocking doors that descended, overlapping one another until the dock was sealed just like lock gates. We sailed from the jetty out into the Hamoaze and gently nosed into the sheds. As we went into the dock the doors closed behind us with a rumble. The first lieutenant, Andrew Richie, said, 'Come on. Come and watch this'.

We walked off the ship and stood at the head of the dock and watched as the dockyard mateys, each armed with a large wooden wedge and mallet. There were long baulks of timber floating in the water between the dock wall and the ship's sides spaced out at intervals. The foreman was standing alongside us holding a small radio and a whistle. He kept talking into the radio and then, at the appropriate point, he looked down at the ship, blew the whistle, and the mallets would swing, knocking in the wedges simultaneously until the ship was upright and secure. The sluices were opened, the water drained out and the ship was high and dry, ready to be worked on. It was such a slick operation.

We went back on board and had tea. I then took my leave of the wardroom and went back to *HMS Drake* and my cabin where I made preparations to visit the other ships. The next 'serial' on my programme was to join *HMS Berwick* at Portland Harbour. *Berwick* was a type 13 Rothsay class frigate, quite old by this time, with an old weapon systems and rather poor accommodation. She was at sea, so I was issued with a rail warrant and caught the train from Plymouth to Weymouth. At Weymouth station I caught a taxi to Portland. I and a midshipman arrived just as *Berwick* was coming in. We took passage in a supply boat which transported the two of us, the mail and other members of the ship's company, out to the ship.

Having climbed the ladder, I was met by the captain who had the courtesy to come down from the bridge to welcome me. It was an extremely kind gesture considering how busy he was. With everyone on board the supply boat peeled away and we proceeded towards Antwerp. The captain of the ship was Commander John Tolhurst and it was the first of three times that I served with him.

It was a grey, gloomy January day and the ship's company settled down for the evening. I was in the wardroom and was introduced to all the officers who were a mixed bunch but whom I liked instantly. There was a great deal of banter and my leg was pulled constantly as they assessed the new addition to the mess. One positive feature of the evening was that each officer offered to show me around his department, invitations which I accepted enthusiastically.

We were on our way to Antwerp, ostensibly for a goodwill visit, but the trip also coincided with a NATO conference. The conference was due to end with a gala dinner on the Saturday at which a naval presence was required and we were 'it' – the entire wardroom.

The following morning my education into what the ship was about and what it was supposed to do began. The tour of instruction put me in good stead for the future.

After saying Morning Prayer in my cabin, I began my exploration of the ship. *Berwick* was a Type 13 antisubmarine frigate. She was quite elderly by this time and the officers' cabins were down below the main passageway, above the fuel tanks, so there was always a smell of fuel oil around. Due to the age of the ship and the conditions, they were classed as substandard cabins, so we received what were called 'Hard Layers', extra payments to compensate for substandard accommodation. The cabins were gloomy, but on a positive note they were private and I was more than happy with mine. The only problem was that the heads and bathroom were one deck up. It meant that to go for a wash or shower we had to negotiate ladders and cross the main 'drag' where the rest of the ship's company were up and down the passageway. It made ablutions a little awkward at times.

One of my first tasks was to visit the police station, or to give it its proper name, 'the regulating office', to see the master-at-arms and get the names of the leading hands and presidents of the messes. I then visited them and said that I hoped it was the first of a number of visits. I added that I would appreciate an invite to the mess to meet the members and to get to know them. To my delight, they all agreed and said they would get back to me.

I continued my exploration of *Berwick* and scrounged a cup of tea in the machinery spaces, a practice that became standard in all the ships in which I served. My wanderings were noticed to such an extent that the chief stoker exclaimed in good humour one day: 'For God's sake, Bish, you're all over the place, like a rash!'

'I've got limited time,' I explained, 'but I'm trying hard to find out how the ship works, who everyone is and where they fit in – hopefully without getting in the way too much.'

We arrived at the mouth of the river Scheldt which is a very wide estuary and proceeded up river to the port of Antwerp. *Berwick* berthed alongside the jetty port side to, and began to prepare for the cocktail party. It took place on the Thursday evening and went very well. Some of the guests came down to the wardroom afterwards and did not leave the ship until late.

When 'leave' was piped the following afternoon, we went ashore. I was in the company of a number of officers who were keen to see what Antwerp was like. The city dates back to the Middle Ages and is famed for its diamond businesses. To my astonishment to get to the city centre we had to pass through an extensive red-light district with all the girls sitting in the windows. I had never seen such a sight, much to the amusement of my companions. I have to say that it did not cause me that much of a problem.

A young midshipman was celebrating his eighteenth birthday and some of the more disreputable members of the wardroom encouraged him to have a few drinks and then tried to arrange a liaison for him. He declined, wise boy.

I had got tired of this nonsense and it was very cold, so I adjourned to a hostelry where in due course I was joined by some of my companions who were freezing too. We were grateful for a warm place where our teeth stopped chattering.

A few minutes passed and into the pub came half a dozen very attractive young ladies; it had suddenly become a 'target rich environment'. As sailors do, we fell into conversation with them and it turned out that they were, what shall we say, 'Ladies of the Night?' and were the night shift! They went on 'duty' at 2100. They were very intelligent and their English was a lot better than our French; in fact, we discovered that one or two of them had attended university and had degrees.

We asked why they followed this line of work and their answer was 'the money'. They couldn't make a living in their preferred careers and had university loans to pay off. They claimed that it was the only way open to them. They were in a cooperative and paid a 'mamasan' to look after the books and supervise the front desk. They divided the rest of their takings equally but had to contribute toward the upkeep of the premises. They each had a shift which rotated, but some girls had their own independent routine. The women told us that there was a doctor's wife who did day shifts. Once her husband had gone to the surgery and the children had been taken to school, she started work and ensured she had finished in time for the return of her family. When we asked why she would do this, the girls told us she was bored with her lot.

It was great talking to them and we learned a great deal. They were such bright, intelligent girls; it's such a pity that that's all they could find in the way of employment. And before you ask, no, we did not avail ourselves of their services.

The NATO dinner in Brussels on the Saturday evening proved unspectacular; so much so, that I can't remember much about it. Not that we were drunk. All I can remember is that we had a minibus to take us there and bring us back to the ship, and we had to be on our best behaviour.

I held services on the Sunday morning and we sailed for home the following day. It was not the greatest run ashore and I was glad to be heading home. It took a few days to get back to Plymouth and it was a delight getting to know the ship's company of *HMS Berwick*.

A number of characters in the wardroom spring to mind. There was 'Jorry' Carrier, a seaman officer; Tony McManus, who was the deputy weapons electrical officer; Tony Syrett, the weapons electrical officer, whose wedding I later undertook at St. Paul's Cathedral; the 'Jimmy' (first lieutenant) was Hamish Lauden; and the captain was John Tolhurst. My first sojourn had been a pleasure and I looked forward to my next time on board *Berwick*.

The next item on my programme was an exercise called 'Spring Train'. The entire Third Flotilla, of which our squadron was a part, was to set sail for the North Atlantic. In total, thirty-one ships were taking part. It was an exercise to test antisubmarine capabilities, air defence and fleet manoeuvres. It was also an opportunity for ship handling skills to be improved. It promised to be a very busy time.

The flotilla was under the command of Rear Admiral Peter Stanford whose flag was flown on *HMS London*, a county class cruiser. When a flag is flown in those circumstances, it indicates that the ship is under the control of a very senior officer. Our squadron was a mixed one with ships of different types and ages. *Antelope*, now out of the maintenance sheds, was a Type 21 frigate, very modern with a large part of her constructed of aluminium. She had a ship's company of about one hundred and fifty men.

We also had two Leander frigates, *Jupiter* and *Aurora*, which had been refitted with Ikara antisubmarine missiles, both with a ship's company of about two hundred and fifty. *Berwick* was a Type 13 frigate fitted with a forward turret of two 4.5-inch guns. She also had Sea Slug wire-guided missiles, anti-submarine mortars and a Wasp helicopter. *Jupiter* was a gun Leander too and she was the leader. The captain was Geoffrey Dalton who I soon got to know very well.

We were due to leave on the Monday morning and on Sunday afternoon, having sorted out my kit after leaving *Berwick,* I joined *Aurora* and was assigned a cabin where I unpacked and stowed my kit away. I spent the first evening on board getting to know the officers and talking to the first lieutenant about my role and how I could fit in on a day-to-day basis.

Late in the evening the navigator came into the wardroom and I liked him instantly. His name was Jonathan Ellison and his father was Bishop of London, but that's not why I liked him. Johnny was a rogue and nothing like you would ever expect a bishop's son to be.

The next morning we sailed from Plymouth to join the flotilla and headed into a Force 4 gale. The weather kept deteriorating and by the time we reached the Western Approaches it was blowing Force 8-9. It was most uncomfortable and Type 21s were poor 'sea boats'. At one point, *Antelope*, which was on our starboard quarter, appeared to be submerged. Conditions on board were not great and most of the one hundred and fifty men were down with seasickness. There were only three officers on their feet. Sea conditions were pretty bad.

The squadron assembled and then promptly scattered to aid merchantmen in peril across the North Atlantic. *Aurora* received a signal to go to the aid of an East German ship. It was in difficulty two hundred miles further out into the Atlantic. The cargo had shifted and she was in trouble. *Aurora's* captain, Jonathan Appleyard-List, came on the main broadcast and informed us of the ship's plight and that we would be turning into the sea. He said it was likely to be a very bumpy night and that we had to make sure that the ship was completely secure for sea. He wasn't kidding, it was a very bumpy night. It was one of the few nights when it was safer to lie in your bunk than to walk around. I strapped myself into my bunk so that I wouldn't roll out because it was a four foot drop to the deck. I only ever had to do that twice during my time in the navy.

The ship shuddered as we ploughed into the sea at our

best possible speed. We were due to make the rendezvous at dawn the following day, but when we reached the appropriate point on the chart, there was no sign of the East German vessel. There was no way that it had passed us in the night because it was visible on the radar – and then it wasn't. They had gone! We searched for survivors, but none were to be found.

We headed back the way we had come, turning across the sea, so the ship heeled horribly. Once we had completed the manoeuvre, we had a 'following sea' which made life a little easier. East of our position – although we didn't know it – *Jupiter*, who had sailed twenty-four hours behind us due to a malfunction in a motor on the tiller flat, had gone to the aid of a Greek merchantman in the Western Approaches. They got there and picked up eleven survivors. The ship had gone down and there were men in life rafts and in the water. Some of those in the water had their life jackets on the wrong way and instead of keeping their heads above the water the jackets were forcing their heads under water.

In the most horrendous sea, *Jupiter*'s diver went into the water to rescue these men. He jumped in on the port side only for the ship to go straight over the top of him. Thankfully, he surfaced on the starboard side. He had to swim around the stern of the ship, avoiding the propellers, to reach the men in the water. He pulled them in one by one and they were hoisted out of the water and rushed to the sick bay. One was taken to the wardroom bathroom. The bath was filled with tepid water and he was plunged into this because he had hypothermia. Sadly, he died. In total four men died which considering the atrocious conditions is amazing. 'For those in peril on the sea' is not a meaningless prayer.

For his courage and determination, *Jupiter's* diver received the Queen's Commendation. That was the least he deserved.

We then assembled as a flotilla and began the exercise. The weather abated slightly and we were able to carry out the exercises and training that were necessary, but it was all under difficult circumstances. I was acting as second officer of the watch on one occasion and was checking our course on the charts. The Atlantic moves from West to East and has great rollers and about every third or fourth one is bigger than the others. We took one of those rollers on the beam on the starboard side and the ship began to roll. Above the chart table on the bridge there is a small board with an arrow on it: this shows the degree of list the ship is experiencing. I called it the 'swingometer' and the maximum it can go to is thirty degrees.

As the ship heeled over, I lost my hand hold and tumbled across the bridge, falling head over heels, followed by charts, pencils and rubbers. The captain, who was in his chair hanging on for grim death, looked at me and said, 'Are you ok?' and I replied that I was.

There was a good number of people on the bridge apart from the duty watch, all hanging on to whatever hand holds they could grab. As I sat with my back against the bulkhead, I could feel the ship continuing to heel and heard the arrow on the swingometer 'clack' against the stop – but she kept going. Those who remained upright said the flying bridge abaft the Ikara well was taking the tops off the waves! The ship was almost on its side. Had she gone any further the sea would have poured into the funnel and she could have turned turtle and capsized.

Gradually, oh so gradually, she righted herself. There

was an audible sigh of relief from everyone and the men got on with their jobs. I gathered up the charts, pencils and rubbers, helped by one of the duty watchmen and carried on where I had left off. It was a salutary reminder that the sea can be a very dangerous place even in a modern warship.

During 'Spring Train' Sundays were a bit different. Although there was some training it was not so intense and usually confined to individual ships. I conducted services in the junior ratings' dining room. The services were reasonably well attended but even sitting down, people had to brace their feet to stop the chairs from sliding about. My legs were braced apart and everything was done 'carefully'. Traditionally, Sunday evening was movie night and we did try to watch a film, but changing the reels and holding on to the projector proved too difficult and we abandoned it.

'Spring Train' lasted approximately two weeks and we did complete all the required training. But with all the ships sustaining storm damage, we proceeded towards Gibraltar for repairs. I will never forget my first glimpse of the African coastline silhouetted against the early morning sun. It might have been my imagination, but I swear I could smell the distant deserts. It was all very romantic and exciting. The warmth of that early morning promised a complete contrast to the ravages of the Atlantic wastes.

80mil mortar

Boom!

Dartmouth Course, post-Damage Control

Helping to build the 'Nuke'

Landing Sardinia

Lympstone 'death slide' my nemesis

Me in uniform for the first time!

Second boom!

Setting up mortars on Sardinia

Setting up the 'Nuke'

Ancient amphitheatre

Base camp at Akamas

Base camp at Akamas, another view

Embarkation

Evensong at Akamas

Going home

Not Samson, just me among Cyprus ruins

Earth Movers! I wasn't allowed to drive!

Rock race

Pause for libation on the road to Akamas

Sunset in the Med

This is called a 'Scraper'

Working on 'Irish' bridge

What a big hole we made!

Alongside in Cadiz

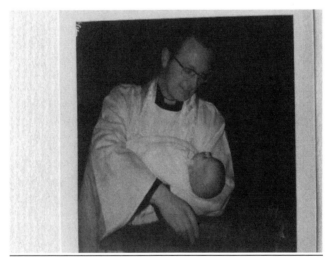

Baptism

Getting ready for Jubilee parade

Green Goddess

Hotel fire

HMS Antelope

HMS Aurora

HMS Berwick

Me in whites

On board HMCS Ottawa

Practising ceremonial

Preaching at sea

Remembrance Sunday

Running into St Petersburg USA

Russian aircraft carrier 'Minsk'

St Petersburg runners

Stanavforlant

HMS Jupiter at Venice

Chapter Seven

A Trip to Venice and a Brush with the Local Carabinieri

Gibraltar promised to be another adventure. It was my first visit, and having read about it and heard so much about it I was really looking forward our stay. The harbour was filled with ships and we were berthed out on the far side of it, the furthest point from the town. To get to the dockyard gate, we had to walk all the way round, but that was fine. Our visit proved illuminating.

I was part of the wardroom of *HMS Aurora* and Jonathan Ellison mischievously suggested that we have a 'vicar's run ashore'. I had half a dozen clerical shirts with me and agreed, on the understanding that any damages would be paid for. It was all arranged, but bit by bit people dropped out. On the Saturday evening, just the two of us went ashore. Jonathan was dressed in a clerical shirt and I disembarked as the navigator in 'dog robbers', that is jacket and tie.

In the very first pub outside the dockyard gate, a sailor in uniform, a submariner, spotted Jonathan and the clerical collar, and came to the bar. He threw his arms around him and exclaimed: 'Thank you for looking after my family.' He repeated it over and over again with tears in his eyes.

Over his shoulder, Jonathan looked at me and mouthed, 'Who is he?'

I shrugged because I hadn't got a clue. All the sailor had seen was the clerical collar. He was obviously grateful to a chaplain who had helped him in the past; he was also very drunk. No sooner had we left one emotional scene than we were confronted with another. At a second bar we saw the wife of the chaplain of Gibraltar in very tearful form. I didn't want to get involved in whatever was bothering her, so we hurriedly left and ended up at the officers' club. We thought our dramas were over for the night. How wrong we were. Jonathan and I headed for the bar where I ordered drinks. No sooner had I done so than the flag lieutenant suddenly appeared in front of us and said the admiral would like to see us. It sounded ominous.

We went over to the table where Rear Admiral Sir Peter Stanford was sitting. He was an imposing figure, very tall and with mutton chop whiskers. He spoke very carefully. He asked why Jonathan was dressed as a chaplain and why I was in civilian clothes. When we told him about our 'vicar's run ashore', he ordered us back to the ship immediately with a flea in our ears.

I asked, 'Please Sir, may we finish our drinks?' which made things worse. I was told not to push my luck.

We headed back to the ship and opened the night bar and had a night cap. We carried on the conversation that we'd been having during our meanderings back through the dockyard. Jonathan said he'd been brought up in the bishop's palace at Chester because father had been the bishop there prior to becoming Bishop of London. He said: 'All my life I have been around clergy of one sort or another, but for the very first time I've realised that by putting this shirt on, you have to be 'Mr Nice Guy' all the time. You have to be nice to everyone otherwise you will lose the role that you have been given.'

It had proved an interesting experience for him, while I saw the other side of things as well. Jonathan had aspirations to go into the world of the Secret Intelligence Service, but I don't think he achieved it. My last contact with him was when I received an invitation to his marriage to a Belgian girl whose father was in the diamond trade. As far as I'm aware he went into the diamond trade himself. Ray Roberts had an invitation too because he had known Jonathan at Dartmouth but neither of us went. By that time, I was an impoverished vicar of a country parish and what could I give a diamond merchant? A pair of M & S towels wouldn't quite cut it! But we sent our very best wishes.

The night bar didn't stay open for too long because I had another move. My programme meant that I had to leave *Aurora* and cross over to *Jupiter* for the next phase of our deployment in the Mediterranean. Early the next morning I packed my belongings, moved out of my cabin, walked along the jetty to *Jupiter* and moved into another cabin in time for us to sail as a squadron for Venice.

At the planning meeting for our Italian visit Captain Dalton had been told that we were to be the only warships in Venice at the time, but when we sailed into the lagoon upon which the great city stands, the shadow of the mighty *USS Eisenhower* fell across us. She had cost $679 million to construct, an enormous sum that would equate to around $4.5 billion today. She was anchored in the middle of the lagoon because this 90,000-ton aircraft carrier couldn't get alongside.

We moved to our berth which was within walking distance of the city centre. It proved a fascinating weekend. Venice is one of the marvels of the world. It's built on one hundred and eighteen small islands and has one hundred and fifty canals. The most spectacular is The Grand Canal which is lined by magnificent churches and palaces. Moving from one part of Venice to another is often done via one of its four hundred bridges.

Dozens of American sailors were strolling around Venice enjoying the sights. The Americans had a procession of Liberty boats bringing personnel into the city and taking them back to their ship. What was extraordinary was that to kill time between the Liberty boats going back and forth, the Americans had set up barbecues on the jetty and telephone boxes, so people could phone the United States free of charge as long as no one overdid it. With typical American generosity, they allowed us to use their telephones to contact our own families. They also offered us as many hot dogs and burgers as we wanted. Inevitably someone will always take advantage of a generous offer and it was a young midshipman, not the brightest of souls. He phoned his girlfriend in Manchester and was on the phone for over half an hour. The American offer of free calls was withdrawn with some embarrassment on our part. The midshipman was in everybody's bad books for some time.

To ensure that their sailors did not get lost, the Americans had painted a trail of footprints from the jetty to Piazza San Marco – St Mark's Square. All the sailors had to do was follow the footprints there and back. I was amazed at this but nevertheless that's what they did. We on the other hand blended into the life of Venice in the manner of British matelots. It's a beautiful city, but early in the year it can be very cold in northern Italy.

During any port visit there are always invitations to functions of one sort or another and usually a list is placed in the messes to inform people that they should attend a particular function. A list went up in the wardroom and one of the invitations was for two officers to accompany the captain to a lunch given by a former ambassador to the Holy See. I think his name was Sir Bernard Brown but I'm open to correction. Nobody wanted to go. Anxious to secure 'volunteers', the first lieutenant leaned on one of the midshipmen to append his name. They wanted one more officer. I hadn't put my name down for anything, so on the spur of the moment I announced, 'I'll go with the captain', and everybody in the wardroom heaved a sigh of relief.

We went to the lunch and received a very warm welcome in a magnificent apartment with good company. One of the advantages of being in the Navy is the opportunity to meet varied and interesting people and so it proved in this case. Sir Bernard and Lady Brown were very attentive and amusing hosts and we did our bit to entertain them. I was sitting next to an elderly lady and during the meal we conversed and I discovered that she was a Contessa; unfortunately, her table manners did not match the lavish surroundings. She didn't finish any of the courses and when she came to the pudding, she lit up a cigarette not in the least concerned as to what the other guests might think. While the conversation hummed around her, she tapped the ash into her pudding and then put the cigarette end into the coffee cup. I thought it was disgusting but smiled sweetly and carried on our conversation. My Italian was non-existent, but her English was reasonable and we were able to discuss a number of topics. She proved to be a fascinating woman despite her table manners.

After lunch we took our leave. The midshipman asked

if he could do some shopping and Captain Dalton gave his permission. The captain and I then strolled back to the ship via the narrow streets and lanes of old Venice. We were in uniform and drew some glances as we browsed in various shops. Geoffrey became a very different man when he was away from the ship. He was more relaxed and a good companion. I got to know him quite well in that short time and latterly when I became chaplain to *HMS Jupiter's* association. Sadly, before the annual reunion in 2020, Geoffrey died, but I hope his widow Lady Jane will continue to grace us with her presence at future events.

On Sunday morning I and a small group of sailors headed for St George's, the Anglican church in Venice. Other members of the crew were taking part in a charity walk. At the cocktail party I had met the church warden of the English church and he had asked if I would preach on the Sunday. The service was entirely in English and we all enjoyed the experience. The congregation were kind enough to provide coffee afterwards and made a fuss of the sailors; it was always nice to be able to support and help local congregations when we could.

The afternoon was a rather different affair. I had a spot of lunch on the ship and then decided to find the post office in Venice, so I could telephone home; it was long before the advent of mobile phones. I went ashore in clerical collar and Pusser's issue raincoat and wandered through the city centre until I found the post office. Inside, a helpful woman who spoke English directed me to a booth and I followed her instructions in how to make an international call. My mother did not have a phone, but my aunt living next door did. As soon as my call got through my cousin ran to fetch my mother. It took a while for her to get to the phone, so we didn't have time for a long conversation, but I did have time to reassure her that all was well.

I never phoned Jeannetta or the children because I used to find it too upsetting. It upset the children knowing that I wasn't coming home. It meant calls home were normally made to my mother who was keen to know that I was okay.

Having made the phone call, I started to stroll back to the ship. All of a sudden, a voice shouted: 'Hiya Bish, come and have a drink.' There were four sailors and a midshipman sitting just inside the open window of a bar.

I leaned on the open sill and said: 'Thanks but I'm heading back to the ship.'

They said: 'Oh come on, we've also got one of the ship's boats and it will be great to see Venice from the water.'

Against my better judgement I went into the bar and had a beer with them. That one drink became several more and by the time we arrived at the mooring it was late afternoon. We climbed aboard and the killick – the leading seaman responsible for the boat – started the engine and we got under way. In winter the lagoon tends to be low which meant there were exposed mudflats. We weren't even sure where we were going and ran aground several times. There was much laughter as we hit another mudflat and ended up in a tangle of arms and legs in the bottom of the boat. To free the bows, we had to jump up and down in the stern. All of this generated a lot of noise which echoed around the buildings. Our inebriated state didn't help matters either. We were disturbing the peace of a Sunday afternoon and, without meaning to, annoyed the local residents.

As we passed under a bridge two members of the Carabinieri shouted out:

'How you say stop Inglesi? Stop, stop!'

We waved back and sang in return, 'Just one cornetto, give it to me.'

The afternoon became an Italian farce as the Carabinieri ran over bridges while we passed underneath them. On and on the game went. It seemed to go on for ages but might have been a few minutes. Eventually we entered the Grand Canal and turned toward the ship. We could her the twittering of the pipes calling 'Sunset'

The killick looked nervous and said: 'I'm in trouble now. The boat should have been returned before this',

As we came alongside, I said, 'Let me go first.'

The lads said, 'You're pulling rank, Bish.' (Senior officers are the first to go into a ship and are last out of it.)

I said: 'Don't be daft, I haven't got any rank to pull, but if you let me go first, we might just get away with it.'

At the top of the ladder was the master-at-arms. I climbed up the ladder and saw his gleaming toe caps and raised my eyes to see him peering at his clipboard.

As I reached the deck he said, 'Name?'

'Wishart.'

He looked up from the clipboard and saw it was the chaplain and walked away muttering a few expletives. If he wasn't prepared to book me, he couldn't really book the others. We had got away with it. It was naughty of me and next the day I went and apologized to him for misusing my position. The boat should not have been out after hours, but, hey ho, that's the adventures of sailors. The master-at- arms invited me to have a cup of tea with him and it all ended amicably – or so I thought. There was an uncomfortable footnote to the story. The following day one of the liaison team asked if I would stand in for him, just for an hour or so, because he wanted to do some shopping. He hadn't been able to get ashore due to liaison duties. Always ready to help, I agreed. The killick who had been in charge of the boat the previous afternoon was on duty too and nearly everyone else had gone ashore. What could go wrong?

Not long afterwards two Carabinieri arrived enquiring whether we had had a boat out the previous afternoon. I consulted the killick and the boat roster and told them that we hadn't had a boat out, but perhaps one of the other ships had. They went off to make enquiries of *Aurora*, *Berwick* and *Antelope*. Eventually they came back saying the other ships had said the same thing: none of their boats had been out on the canals the previous afternoon. I assured him that it wasn't us and they left scratching their heads and arguing among themselves. To my shame, I told a lie because I thought we hadn't done any harm, apart from being a nuisance, and it saved the ship from what could have been a diplomatic embarrassment. I also avoided a severe dressing down. To this day, whenever I visit Italy, I always look at the Carabinieri with jaundiced eyes wondering if they're coming to arrest me.

After our visit to Venice came to an end, we continued our deployment in the Mediterranean with a spot of espionage. A signal came in saying that the new Russian aircraft carrier the *Minsk* had sailed out of the Black Sea and was in the Mediterranean. She was accompanied by a number of escort ships. We were deployed to find her and photograph her.

W discovered that she was anchored near Crete.

115

Antelope, by far the fastest ship in the squadron, was dispatched ahead to see if it could find her exact position. They found her and when we arrived, all the ship's helicopters were launched to photograph this new addition to the Soviet fleet. Our actions annoyed them, but since they were in Greek waters and Greece was a member of NATO, there was nothing they could do about it. We sent them greetings and carried on our way.

Chapter Eight

Behind the Iron Curtain and in the Lair of a Dictator

Our next port of call was Istanbul. As we approached the Turkish coast, I reflected on the fact that adventures were coming thick and fast. We anchored in the Golden Horn which is a stretch of water between Asia and Europe. Istanbul spans the waterway. It is an amazing city and on my first visit it was unbelievably exciting to wake in the morning at anchor in the Golden Horn and hear the cry of the muezzins from the minarets in a plethora of mosques calling the faithful to prayer. It was something that I'd heard and seen on television and in the cinema but I never thought I'd see or experience such things, which is one good reason to join the navy.

Our duties in Istanbul were primarily of a goodwill nature; a squadron of British warships calling on a NATO ally. During the visit we were entertained by members of the Turkish Navy. The usual cocktail party was held on the Thursday evening and the embassy staff came down from Ankara to attend it along with members of staff at the consulate in Istanbul. Expatriates, local dignitaries, and local businessmen and their wives were also entertained.

Some of our people had already gone ashore to explore the delights of Turkey, but my adventure had to wait until the next afternoon when 'leave' was piped. Going into the

Grand Bazaar and the Spice Bazaar was truly amazing. The vast array of shops and stalls was breathtaking. There was a ceaseless hubbub of voices calling out invitations to come and see their wares. The smells of a hundred spices, oranges and all kinds of fruit, filled the air making it a heady experience.

The Grand Bazaar is a wonderful shopping opportunity and sailors like to take gifts home, perhaps to assuage the feelings of guilt that whilst we are away enjoying ourselves our families bear the brunt of separation. I was no exception and when we left home, blouson leather jackets were all the rage so, having written home for sizes, I bought three leather jackets for my children and a three quarter length suede coat for my wife. By the time we got home fashions had changed and my daughters rarely wore theirs. Trials and tribulations! Nevertheless, I absorbed the atmosphere of a city which until that point had only existed in my imagination or in the pages of history or travel books. I visited Topkapi Palace, a large museum which was once the residence of the Ottoman sultans, and enjoyed a full tour of the city and all its attractions.

The greatest disappointment for me was that because Turkey was a Muslim country I was not able to go ashore in clerical collar. I had to do everything in collar and tie or civilian clothes. When I went to the consulate to conduct a service for them, I had to carry my clothes, robes and communion set in a grip, and change there. My memory of that initial visit is hazy. I remember climbing into the back of a taxi to go to an official function in uniform, but I could not wear clerical collar. I had to wear a collar and tie. The taxi had a strip of metal along the back of the seats near the floor and as I got out the toe cap on my new naval shoes caught on the metal strip and was cut across. I was really annoyed with myself. It's funny the things that stick in your mind. Despite the mishap, that pair of shoes lasted me for years.

On 21 March, we sailed from Istanbul into the Black Sea via the Dardanelles. We were bound for the Romanian port of Constanta where we were due to arrive on 23 March. Transiting the Dardanelles was a salutary experience for many of us. We were a short distance from the shore and could see the site of the Battle of Gallipoli. It was a moving experience. I tried to gain some sort of imaginary picture of what it must have been like for those soldiers and sailors of the First World War. All of them would have been around our age. What difficulties, hardships and horrors had they faced? But I found it impossible to imagine. Through binoculars, the shoreline looked so peaceful in the spring sunshine, it was hard to visualise the slaughter that took place there.

We entered the Black Sea where we were instantly shadowed by a Soviet 'AGI', an intelligence gathering trawler bristling with antenna. We knew exactly what it was and I'm sure they knew all about us. The Soviets followed us into the port and when we berthed alongside, they were berthed astern and ahead of us. No doubt they were examining the hull to gain whatever information they could. We remained in Constanta until 26 March, during which time we were involved in a number of goodwill activities.

At the time Romania was suffering under the evil regime of Nicolae Ceaușescu, a communist and Stalinist dictator, and there was the risk of contrived incidents – such as the usual pantomime during the ship's 'postcard run'. Once the gangway was down someone, usually me, went ashore to get postcards which could be sent with the mail before we moved on. In Constanta I had a midshipman called Roger for company. We found a kiosk and bought postcards and stamps for those who wanted them in the wardroom and headed back to the ship. Suddenly, a seedy looking chap sidled up to us, asking to exchange money at an exceptionally good rate of exchange. We politely declined because this was a classic 'sting'. If we had accepted the offer, we could have been accused of laundering foreign currency. That would have led to an arrest and a diplomatic incident. We didn't fall for it and just carried on back to the ship with our postcards. Roger muttered, 'Pity it wasn't a honey trap!'

That evening a reception was held on board *Antelope*. There were two reasons she was chosen to host the event: she had a wider wardroom than the other vessels which meant she could accommodate more people, and she was renowned for having the best food in the squadron. A selection of officers from the other ships were there to help with the hosting or 'mingling'. We had a visit from naval intelligence, who gave a briefing just before the guests arrived indicating the kind of questions we should ask and the sort of things to look out for, so that we could glean useful information from the visit.

The Cold War was at its height and we were keen to obtain details such as how much the Romanian Navy had developed or whether the Soviet Navy had expanded in the Black Sea. The guests were the usual mix local dignitaries but included a number of Romanian naval officers and their wives. Judging by the numbers, *Antelope* was the most popular venue in Romania that night. On one occasion during the evening, I was completely surrounded by a number of wives of Romanian naval officers who were deeply concerned about the spiritual development of their children. Because we were on board a British warship, I was able to wear clerical collar as part of my uniform and they spotted this and zoomed in on me.

They were concerned that most of the churches had been closed in Romania. There was one Roman Catholic church that remained open in Constanta, but we learned a few weeks later that it had been closed too. I was unable to reassure these good ladies but could only recommend prayer and political action.

During the course of the evening, I fell into conversation with a Romanian naval officer who didn't speak English. We conversed a little bit in German or by sign language. I noticed that his glass was empty, so I asked if he wanted another drink. He said 'Vassar', so I went to the bar to get him a glass of water, but a naval intelligence officer intervened and said, 'I'll get that.' I suspect the officer added vodka or something because after two glasses the Romanian naval officer miraculously discovered the ability to speak English.

I remember the phrase that he used until my dying day. He said: 'The freedom loving people of Romania have no aggressive inclinations towards the West, however we are building a new destroyer complex in the cliffs further south.' Our people were making mental notes and almost saying: 'Hold on George, let's get that down on paper!' It was stunning information. Within a couple of minutes two Romanian men dressed in smart suits came off the bulkhead, where they had been observing proceedings with folded arms, and announced, 'He is not well.' They marched him out of the door, across the deck and down the gangway. He was bundled into a black Mercedes in which the curtains were closed and he was driven away.

I've often wondered about that man. Yes, it was our duty to find out what we could about their navy, but I wonder whether getting him drunk caused him and his family serious trouble and possibly the loss of his life. Ceaușescu was a brutal dictator who used his secret police, the Securitate, to instil fear in the population.

Just over a decade later, in 1989, there was an uprising and he ordered the military to open fire on protesters. It led to many deaths and injuries. The military then changed sides and executed Ceaușescu and his wife by firing squad. It was poetic justice for an evil man who had been prepared to use violence against his own people.

At that time the port of Constanta was a very down-at-heel city, but I have no idea as to its condition now. There were many incomplete buildings; other buildings were in desperate need of repair; pavements were broken and there were potholes everywhere. I was baffled as to how anyone could imagine that the communist system worked. After the fall of the regime great evils were uncovered such as the treatment of orphans and abandoned children. Ceaușescu worked on the Stalinist principle that the more people you had in your population the better your economy would perform. But in reality, it doesn't work because it means not everybody is able to have a sustainable job. The state encouraged the population to have children, but parents struggled to support them and often abandoned them. These children ended up in appalling circumstances which came to light after the regime was overthrown.

Our visit was subject to draconian restrictions. We were forbidden to hire cars even though there weren't any. We weren't allowed to go on the trains and we were even banned from using bikes. In other words, we were stuck in Constanta and the dockyard area. Having said that, the skills, ingenuity and downright cheek of sailors never ceases to amaze me. Two of our petty officers managed to go ashore in uniform, went to the railway station and hopped on a train. They alighted from the train several stops down the track. What then took place was reminiscent of a scene from the film 'The Guns of Navarone' in which German soldiers arrive at a wedding party where an Allied commando unit have secreted themselves among the guests.

Our two petty officers were walking down the road of this small town when a wedding procession came round the corner and came to an abrupt halt at the sight of two men in uniform. Quick as a flash, one of the officers plucked a rose from a nearby garden, stepped forward and handed it to the bride with a flourish and saluted. The wedding party erupted with joy, seized the two naval officers and escorted them enthusiastically into the reception. They were having a great time until the Securitate arrived and arrested the petty officers.

Members of the Romanian Navy later handed them over to the ship along with a vociferous complaint. The captain of the ship swore he would hand out the most severe punishment possible and a diplomatic incident was avoided. When the representatives of the Romanian Navy had gone, the two petty officers were reminded that we were guests in a foreign country and should behave according to their rules. Wrists slapped, everybody fell about laughing and the two petty officers were congratulated on their style and charm which were in the true traditions of the service. Their actions had reflected our open democratic system and enabled them to make contact with some of the local people.

Constanta was a miserable place to visit and would never be considered a good run ashore – or any kind of run ashore. On Saturday and Sunday afternoon and evening every mess deck showed movies. The screenings were packed out because no one wanted to go into Constanta. Our visit was an education into what life was like in countries behind the Iron Curtain and China.

My time in *Jupiter* had come to an end and before sailing I gathered my possessions and moved to *Antelope* for the run home. The return journey took in stops at Gibraltar, Cadiz, and Lisbon where *Antelope* would spend Easter. We sailed on 26 March and proceeded west along the Black Sea, the way we had come. We transited the Dardanelles again and sailed out into the Golden Horn at Istanbul, but this time we weren't stopping.

I was deemed the 'entertainment officer' and not long after leaving Constanta, Captain Pat Rowe had sent for me. He said: 'After that bloody awful place, the morale of the ship's company is low. How are we going to get it back up?'

The captain expected me to come up with a few morale-boosting ideas and I was at a loss as to how to approach the request. I went to the 'Fount of all Knowledge', the chief petty officer's mess and talked to the men there.

The first suggestion was an upper deck barbecue and horse racing evening, but because we were in a squadron, permission had to be gained from the lead ship, *Jupiter,* before this could be done. The captain signalled *Jupiter* seeking permission, but it was denied. Captain Dalton explained that because we were transiting the Black Sea and being shadowed, we didn't want to give the Russians the idea that we were all at play.

Captain Pat then said to me: 'We'll wait until we break company with *Jupiter* and the others and then we'll have the upper deck barbecue and horse racing. Until then, think again. See what you can come up with.'

I returned again to the chief petty officer's mess for inspiration, and the suggestions to brighten the mood of gloom were a fish and chip evening and sod's opera. A sod's opera is a variety show with mess decks entertaining each other. It would take place in the junior ratings' dining hall and be out of sight. The captain nodded his approval and the word went out. It was to be held on the Saturday night. The cooks were delighted because it meant that supper would be in newspaper and it was a simple menu for everyone. The only people who 'dipped out' were those on watch.

The dining hall was rigged with a stage, extra beer was issued and we got ready for a good night's entertainment. I acted as compere. We had Frank Sinatra impressions, singers and comedians. We had a 'Miss Antelope Competition' which was won by an eighteen-year-old stoker who was forever in trouble. That was because he was such a pretty looking lad that whenever he went ashore, he tried hard to be a rugged, tough, macho man. It led to punch-ups galore. He was so good looking in a pretty way that some people assumed he was gay. He wasn't, but there were those who began teasing him or trying to 'trap' him and that's when the trouble began.

As compere, I had the task of interviewing the 'girls' in our 'Miss Antelope Competition'. It was hilarious when they had beards behind a yashmak and a hairy chest sticking out of a false bra. When I asked them what their ambitions were, the reply would come in a deep voice: 'I'd

125

like to work with children' or 'I'd like to thank my mum for helping me to get here. It's such an honour to take part' and so on. It was a hoot, but it was always a mystery where the sailors got the flimsy female clothes from. They claimed they got them from the rag box that comes from the dockyard, but I wonder. I can't see a suspender belt and other such items being classed as rags. The evening progressed with gusto and finished with a rousing sing song. One of the chiefs was well known for singing sea shanties and other songs, he had his guitar and led the way. Morale was duly lifted.

The following morning, we had church in the junior ratings' dining hall where the entertainment had taken place the previous evening. A good number turned up to sing hymns, led by the previous evening's guitarist. Most received the Sacrament as we proceeded our way westward. It proved a fairly uneventful passage; we touched in at Gibraltar to refuel, and visited Cadiz. We arrived on 4 April which happened to coincide with the four hundredth anniversary of Drake's sacking of the town, so we were not terribly popular.

Cadiz was not a popular run because everyone's mind was on getting home. But there was one incident which surprised me. A few of us went into a bar and we were accosted by an official beggar. It appeared those who were destitute could apply for a licence and be granted 'official beggar status' because the woman had a box with a municipal badge on it. A policeman in the bar quickly hustled her out. I never thought I'd see beggars in western Europe and yet forty years later there are more beggars in Britain than you can shake a stick at.

The squadron set sail for Britain without us. We left Cadiz on 9 April. *Antelope* was scheduled to visit Lisbon as part of her programme and she separated from the squadron and moved up the River Tagus on a goodwill visit to the city. It was my first visit to Lisbon and it is such a beautiful city. As we transited the River Tagus, we passed the magnificent Padrão dos Descobrimentos, Monument of the Discoveries, which celebrates the Portuguese Age of Discovery in the fifteenth and sixteenth century. It is a striking and impressive series of sculptures, depicting thirty-three people from the Age of Discovery, including explorers such as Vasco da Gama, Bartolomeu Dias and Ferdinand Magellan. It is amazing that a small country like Portugal produced such wonderful seafarers who travelled so far and discovered so much of the world. Following the Age of Discovery, almost overnight, the Portuguese navigator seemed to just drop off the map and Portugal ceased to be a major seafaring nation. Nobody knows why.

We came alongside in Lisbon and enjoyed the hospitality offered to us. We arrived on Tuesday in Holy Week. A cocktail party was held on the Thursday and I was invited to celebrate and preach at the embassy church in Lisbon. On Easter Day, I held services on board and then a good number of the crew accompanied me to the church which was huge.

The regular congregation comprised members of the British Embassy staff and members of other embassies such as the United States, Canada, Australia, and so on. The church was packed. It was a great honour and privilege to be able to preach an Easter Sunday sermon to this gathering and be part of that service. We were then entertained to lunch by the embassy staff and enjoyed a delightful time. They went out of their way to make a fuss of the sailors.

Arrangements were made to show the crew around Lisbon and the surrounding area. The weather was warm and sunny and it was a memorable Easter Day. Having said that, a serious incident took place during our visit which involved a number of our sailors who had gone swimming off the beaches at Cascais. They had had too much to drink and one of them dived off the rocks, hit his face a glancing blow and the impact took his nose off. He came out the water laughing but with his nose dangling. His mates had enough common sense to grab him, lay him down and put the nose back to where it was and covered it over. He was rushed back to the ship. We were due to sail two days later and didn't want to leave him behind, so it was decreed that we would paint out the colours on the helicopter and fly him directly to the naval hospital in Gibraltar. I think we broke international agreements by flying across Spanish airspace. At the time Spain and Britain were not talking to each other. They got him to the hospital without incident and the surgeons were able to stitch his nose back on without too much difficulty. He had plastic surgery later and was soon in good form, but a harsh lesson had been learned.

On our return to Plymouth, *Antelope* was 'paying off' which means going in for a refit. The ship would be in the hands of the dockyard and the ship's company would disperse. So, before we left Portugal, the wardroom decided to use up its residual funds on a slap-up meal at a restaurant called 'The Pigadore' in Cascais. The venue was booked and we arrived only to find that they were not ready for us. We sat outside and had drinks and bread and olives.

When they were ready, they took us up to the top floor which had been allocated for our group. We had a delightful meal – medallions of beef with a variety of vegetables and Black Forest gateau to follow. All washed down by twelve bottles of wine. There were only a dozen of us and the price came to a ridiculous £60. A fiver each. We didn't even use up the wardroom funds. We also had a pewter tankard as a keepsake. The chief's mess went to the Holiday Inn and had a black-tie dinner. A glass of sherry cost them £1 which was quite a lot at the time. It pays to shop around.

We sailed from Lisbon on Easter Monday and arrived in Plymouth two days later. Before the ship was paid off there was a 'family day'. This is when the families of the ship's company are taken out to sea for the day. Jeannetta and the children had come down to Plymouth and were staying with friends. Robert was chaplain to commando forces at the Royal Citadel and a great friend.

John was still a very small boy. I had been away for several months and it was with great delight that I tiptoed into his bedroom to see him as he slept. On my first day back the girls were reluctant to go to bed but were pacified by the gifts I had brought them. The following morning Robert drove us to the ship and we set sail for a voyage lasting a few hours. Lunch was served on board and the girls loved exploring the ship. John was too small to appreciate it and was uncertain as to who this man was who was lugging him around. We came back alongside in the afternoon and Robert picked us up. The following morning we returned to Swansea.

There was a footnote to our stay. In those days strawberries were only available in the summer months. None were around in Britain in April, but they were in Portugal. I had brought back several punnets of strawberries and stored them in Robert's fridge. When we got home the phone rang and it was Robert to tell me that we had forgotten the strawberries, but they had been delicious.

Chapter Nine

A Dilemma over my Future

Jeannetta, the children and I went off on a delayed Easter leave which was lovely. Nothing particularly special was done, just the round of visiting friends and relatives, and spending time with the children. Having our own house in Swansea meant we did not stay with my mother. We were able to travel and see friends and go to the parks and all the other things that we enjoyed without impinging on my mother's time and generosity. In fact, we were able to entertain her and she came with us on a number of outings.

The children were back at school before my leave was over, but that was okay because it meant I could carry on and do some jobs around our house and my mother's home. I also came under a great deal of pressure to decide whether I was staying in the Navy or leaving to go back to parish life. Arthur Howells, our local vicar, was keen that I should consider returning to parish life and, as I explained earlier, the seeds had already been sown. I missed the children terribly and the continuity of parish life was something that I wanted to explore again. Chaplaincy is the cutting edge of evangelism because you are dealing with young people who are mainly agnostic, many of whom have never been inside a church. Of course, you are also supporting those who already have a faith and have been Christians for a long time. I had a young family to think about and all these considerations were buzzing round in my mind during my leave period.

In addition to Arthur's prompting, the Bishop of Swansea and Brecon, Benjamin 'Binny' Vaughn, had let it be known that he wanted me to come back to the diocese. There was a parish available in the north of the diocese. A deeply rural one called Beguildy with Heyope. During the leave period we travelled up to Radnorshire to see the outgoing incumbent, Elwyn John. We talked at length about the parish and its attributes. It had a church school for example. By the time my leave ended my mind was in turmoil but I was more or less resigned to leaving the Navy when my four-year short service commission was completed.

But that day had not yet arrived and this time, instead of heading back to Plymouth, I went to Portsmouth because I was due to join *HMS Ariadne* in a few weeks' time. She was part of a NATO squadron, the Standing Naval Force Atlantic (known as STANAVFORLANT). They wanted the services of an education officer as well as a chaplain, so I had to go to Portsmouth and do a short course on education and resettlement. This primarily meant finding courses for people when they were leaving the service. At the time the navy was trying to shed people in what was termed 'premature voluntary release' and to encourage them to take courses which helped them retrain for life in 'civvy street'. The main part of this course was knowing where to find such courses and how to apply for them. In addition, I did a NAMET course, 'Naval Maths and English Test', and the beginnings of O-level English. On joining my new ship, I was now equipped to play an expanded role in the ship's daily routine.

The course was due to last five days and I reported for duty to the naval base *HMS Nelson* on the Sunday afternoon and booked into the wardroom. Little did I realise that I was to see much more of *Nelson* in the years to come. The course was held in the education block and at the end of it I returned home to Swansea, armed with paperwork, files and instructions booklets on all aspects of the courses that I had studied.

I had the weekend at home and then travelled to Fishguard to join *HMS Jupiter.* She had been off the coast of Aberporth testing weapons and was due to make her way to Bayonne in south west France. I caught the train from Swansea and travelled to Fishguard where I arrived early and had to wait for the ship to come in. I was entertained right royally by the local customs officers prior to the arrival of *Jupiter.* Once she had come alongside and was secured, I joined her and we sailed the following morning.

By now I knew Captain Geoffrey Dalton very well and he asked whether I would recommend sailing inside or outside the reef which runs along part of the Pembrokeshire coast. Truthfully, I had no idea, but Geoffrey was a great fan of sea birds and the coast of Pembrokeshire is a haven for breeding grounds.

I said: 'If you want to get close to the birds, I would come inside the reef.'

Geoffrey asked the navigator to plot a new course which was more complicated and it was clear the navigator did not approve of my selection. *Jupiter* sailed carefully inside the reef and to Geoffrey's delight he saw thousands of seabirds and he wasn't the only one taking photographs.

Having transited the reef, we set a course for Bayonne which has naval base facilities and an extensive dockyard. This was part of a goodwill visit that had been planned for some time and there were a number of activities and functions that we were there to fulfil. At the same time we were in Bayonne, *HMS Sheffield* was in Bordeaux as part of British Week. The ships were there to advertise Britain and all that Britain could offer south western France by way of trade.

A football match was arranged between the two ships as part of British Week and we were allocated the local football club's ground to play on. The local community in Bordeaux went out of their way to ensure that we were given a good reception and the game was advertised locally. Ninety per cent of *Jupiter*'s ship's company travelled to Bordeaux to support the team. There was a very good crowd and not just sailors but lots of locals too. The mayor of Bordeaux made a welcoming speech and the game kicked off. We won 3-1 and the ship's company was in full voice singing, '*Leanders last a little bit longer, Leanders are a little bit stronger*'. This was prophetic in many ways because *Sheffield* was lost during the Falklands Campaign and the Leanders that took part sustained hits but survived.

We returned to the ship in good spirits and looking forward to a peaceful evening. But later on an incident took place which lives long in my memory. After the evening meal in the wardroom, I decided to go to bed relatively early. I had some letters to write and wanted to have a read. I had just got into my bunk when there was a knock on the door.

I said, 'Come in.'

Squadron Engineer John Fury, a very proper naval officer and a thunderingly nice man, stood straddling the combing and said: 'There's been an incident on board and a sailor has gone AWOL. Will you come down to the wardroom?'

I dressed hurriedly and went to the wardroom, not knowing what the incident was or why my involvement was required. I discovered there had been a fight on a mess deck. Under the influence of beer, some scurrilous claims had been made about the navigator. The navigator's yeoman took exception to this and thumped the sailor who happened to be a leading hand and senior rating in charge of the mess. The man who did the thumping had also imbibed a quantity of beer and was convinced his naval career was over. The navy takes a dim view of those who strike someone senior to them. Not wishing to end up in 'the rattle' he'd done a runner. Grabbing his coat, he had gone up onto the flight deck and before anyone could stop him, he crossed over the gangway and was away into the darkness beyond.

The uproar that he left behind in the mess deck had been swiftly transmitted to the wardroom where the officer of the day was an Australian called Graham Hascombe. Graham asked me: 'Can you go and find him?'

I said: 'The dockyard is enormous. It's 2300 now. How am I supposed to find him in the dark?'

'But will you try?'

'Yes, of course I'll try.'

I asked one of his colleagues who was standing outside the wardroom door to go to the mess deck and bring me two cans of beer. He shot off and was soon back with them. I put them in my pockets and made my way up onto the flight deck and towards the gangway. On my way I

135

saw Graham again and said: 'I'll try and bring him back. If I do, I don't want him 'trooped'. He won't come back with me if he knows he's going to be severely punished.'

He nodded, 'I'll see what I can do'.

There were about half a dozen people on the flight deck at the time and I borrowed a torch from one of them. I went over the gangway and wandered into the darkness. It was just like it's depicted in films: a pool of light beside the ship and inky blackness beyond. My torch was pretty useless. I fell over some railway lines and discarded pieces of metal as I called out his name, 'Nobby! Nobby! Where are you?'

I shouted out his name a dozen or so times and then out of the darkness a voice said, 'I'm over here Bish.'

I made my way toward the sound of his voice. He was sitting on a wall and gazing at the ship in the middle distance. I clambered up beside him, gave him a tin of beer, which by now was more froth than anything else, pulled out a packet of cigarettes and offered him one. We sat there and smoking and drinking for a few quiet moments.

'Why did you do it Nobby?'

He explained that he'd been angered by the comments made about the navigator.

'Okay, so where are you going to go?'

'Paris.'

'Why Paris?'

'Nottingham Forest are playing there tomorrow evening and I thought I'd make my way there because my mates will help me to get home'.

'Good thinking,' I said. 'Have you got your passport?'

'No'.

'Do you have any money?'

'No'.

'How far do you think you're going to get without your passport? You're not even going to get outside the dockyard gates. If you don't come back with me the local gendarmerie will be informed and you will be arrested and brought back. You'll be guaranteed to spend time in DQs and then dismissed the service.'

What I had said was absolutely true. If he tried to make a run for it, he'd get caught and end up in naval detention quarters.

I said, 'Don't you like the navy?'

'I do.'

'Do you want to leave?'

'No.'

'Well, come back with me'.

He shook his head: 'They'll throw the book at me; I struck a superior rating.'

'Trust me. Come back with me and all will be well. You may get a slap on the wrist, but you won't go to jail.'

After a few moments of thought he agreed. We climbed down from the wall and made our way back to the ship. When we got to the edge of the pool of light I said: 'You're on your own now. You have to go up the gangway under your own steam.' It was important to demonstrate that his return was a voluntary act and that he wasn't drunk.

He went up the gangway without help from me and when he got to the top he stood to attention. The Officer of the Day, Graham Hascombe said: 'In my opinion this man is not under the influence of alcohol. Get below!'

By this time word had got around and the flight deck was full of people waiting to see what would happen. Gradually they broke up and returned to their mess decks.

137

Graham said to me, 'Nice one Bish.'

I returned to the wardroom and reported to the first lieutenant that the man was back on board and adjourned to my cabin. I undressed and climbed back into my bunk. Not long afterwards there was a knock on the door and I thought, not again. It was the killick of the mess deck inviting me down for a drink to say 'thank you' for getting their mess mate back on board with minimal fuss.

The captain never knew about the incident and the miscreant was given five days number 9s at the first lieutenant's table which meant extra duties and loss of leave. His naval career had been saved and there was no loss of face. It was just another evening in the life of a naval chaplain. The remainder of our time in Bayonne was uneventful and we sailed for home, arriving in Portsmouth on 31 May.

Chapter Ten

A Journey to the New World

I left *Jupiter* and went to my cabin in *HMS Drake* to prepare for the next serial in my programme. A few days were spent washing and ironing my kit and packing it ready for the journey to Amsterdam where I was to join *HMS Ariadne* which was part of Standing Naval Force Atlantic.

Ships from NATO countries patrolled northern waters constantly. My warrant took me by train from Plymouth to Harwich and by ferry from Harwich to the Hook of Holland. From the Hook, I boarded a train to Amsterdam. I was met at the station by a midshipman in a car belonging to the Dutch Navy because I had quite a lot of kit including a guitar. We arrived at the port and my bags were taken on board. I immediately called on the captain and the ops officer. My cabin had been allocated and my bags were already in there when I had completed all my other calls.

By this time, it was late afternoon and I was anxious to unpack, shower and change and go down to the wardroom for supper. Many of my colleagues were going ashore and kind enough to invite me, but I declined. I had little in the way of foreign currency and I didn't want to ask people for loans at this stage of the evening because the ship's office was closed.

We sailed the following morning and went through various locks and out into the North Sea. The squadron assembled and carried out 'officer of the watch manoeuvres' as we proceeded towards the English Channel and on to the Atlantic. We passed Plymouth in a misty haze in the early evening. First Lieutenant Charles Freeman intrigued me by saying: 'If you want to see a very pissed off ship's company, come with me'.

I was puzzled by his remark and followed him onto the flight deck where the entire ship's company had gathered watching the city of Plymouth slowly glide past. They stood in total silence. As I turned away a chief petty officer looked at me, shook his head and said, 'Bish, I could f…ing well cry', and walked away.

I discovered later that the squadron commanding officer, an American called Jerry Carter, had sent a signal to *Ariadne* which read: 'Why don't you steam on ahead and have the weekend at home and catch up with us in the Azores?' which garnered the pompous reply, '*HMS Ariadne* will do her duty'.

Ariadne was the longest serving ship with STANAVFORLANT and had been in the squadron for eleven months. She hadn't been in her home port for the entire time, so you can understand the reaction of the ship's company as they gazed at Plymouth with such longing.

I crossed swords with the captain on a number of occasions during the course of the deployment. *Ariadne* was a very unhappy ship. To deliberately ignore Plymouth when the ship's company could have enjoyed a long weekend at home was galling and set the tone for the next three months. I earned my pennies on this deployment. We sailed into the Western Approaches in company with the remainder of the NATO squadron under the command of Commodore Carter and reached the Azores.

Ariadne docked at the NATO fuel jetty on the main island of Santa Margerita. A funny incident took place when a bowser pulled up on the jetty with a consignment for the *Da Silva,* a Portuguese frigate. Out of the vehicle stepped a driver in a greasy cloth cap and vest, with a cigarette dangling from the corner of his mouth. He wandered onto the flight deck of the *USS Koontz* which was the flagship. The officer of the day was a very exact chap; indeed, Americans are very particular about their ships. The officer ordered the driver to throw the cigarette over the side and asked what he wanted. He said he had a consignment for the *Da Silva* who was outboard of (on the other side of) the *Koontz.*

De Silva's officer of the day came across and spoke to the driver and eventually a hose was laid across the *Koontz's* flight deck from the bowser to the *Da Silva.* The hose wasn't long enough to reach in one go and had to be joined to another length of hose. The driver, by now on the jetty, opened a collapsible chair, took out his newspaper, lit a cigarette and began to hand pump the contents of the bowser over to the *da Silva.* About an hour later the officer of the day on the deck of the *Koontz* saw a pool of liquid forming under the joint in the hose. It looked like aviation fuel and he was alarmed. He bent down and sniffed it. He then took off his white glove, put his finger on the pool of liquid and tasted it. It was not aviation fuel; it was red wine. The *da Silva* was taking one thousand gallons of red wine on board. This displeased the Americans whose ships are dry. Assured that the leak would be cleaned up, the officer of the day was duly mollified.

While in harbour I did the rounds of the different ships and spoke to various nationalities, most of whom spoke English except the Portuguese. I met another chaplain in the squadron, a Roman Catholic called Jan Hanne. He was a delightful man and became a great friend. His English was better than mine and he was a Jesuit. The *da Silva* was sailing across the Atlantic and wanted a chaplain on board. I couldn't take services for them because my Latin was non-existent, so Jan left the Dutch ship and went with the *da Silva*. I was approached by the Canadians who asked whether I would join them on *HMCS Ottawa*. Commodore Carter gave his approval and the captain of *Ariadne* wasn't really fussed one way or the other, so I gathered up my possessions and moved over to the *Ottawa* for the crossing of the Atlantic.

Once all the ships had refuelled we sailed from the Azores and headed west towards Bermuda. My time on board was extremely interesting and the Canadians were welcoming and kind. The armed forces in Canada had endured a traumatic experience at the time because the government had decided that they would amalgamate the armed forces into one fighting force. It was a foolish experiment. They all had the same colour uniforms of dark bottle green. Chief petty officers were now warrant officers, petty officers were sergeants, and leading hands were now corporals. The experiment was doomed to failure. To integrate three specialized services into one force was a non-starter. All the servicemen hated it and it caused great confusion. The Canadian Navy later went back to navy blue uniforms and their original ranks. The experiment lasted a few years, but by the time I was on board *Ottawa* there were rumblings that things were going to return to earlier traditions. But during my stay I had to get used to unfamiliar uniforms and different rank structure.

I slept in the sick bay; not ideal, but it worked. I was able to get around the ship and talk to the sailors. On Sunday we had a service on the quarterdeck and they had a rock/country and western band on board, made up of sailors which played the hymns I wanted. They practiced on Saturday afternoons. Following church there was a barbecue for lunch, and afterwards, in extremely relaxed style, they had a sod's opera. I really enjoyed my time with them, especially after they found out that my brother Colin and his family lived in a small village called Angus just outside Toronto.

We were the first ship to arrive at Ireland Island, Bermuda, and berthed alongside. I was in the wardroom and having a cup of coffee with my Canadian colleagues when the first lieutenant strode in and said: 'Anybody want to go to Canada for the weekend?' There was an amazed look on people's faces as they gazed at one another.

The first lieutenant explained that a Boeing 747 transporting military families back to Canada had landed in Bermuda. A routine check had revealed that one of the engines had a fault. The aircraft was grounded until a spare could be flown out. The Canadian families had gone home by scheduled airlines and the 747 had to wait. A Hercules transport plane had brought a new engine out and it was being fitted. The Hercules was waiting for the duff engine to be loaded and its crew had heard that the *Ottawa* was in harbour and, having spare capacity, had offered to take people up to Canada if they wanted a lift home. It would be for a long weekend.

The first lieutenant looked at me and said: 'Your

brother lives in Toronto. Would you like to go up and see him?'

Of course, I was keen, but Colin and I had arranged that he and his wife Joan would come down to Norfolk, Virginia, to see me for a week. However, it was too good an opportunity to miss, so I said: 'I have to get in touch with *Ariadne*,' which I duly did.

The captain gave me permission to go, but it did not go down well with other members of the wardroom. It was understandable. They had been with STANAFORLANT for eleven months and had had very little leave and here was the chaplain, just after joining, off to see his family. There was a lot of grumbling and moaning. It was a great opportunity for me and I think underneath they could see that.

I went over to *Ariadne*, found my passport, hastily threw a few things into my suitcase, and went back to the *Ottawa*. A lift was waiting to take me and two other guys to the airport where we joined the Hercules. The flight went north to the Canadian air base at Trentham. The Hercules is a very noisy aircraft and we had to wear ear defenders which had tiny speakers in them, so we could hear the flight deck conversations. When we were in Canadian air space, the captain of the aircraft received a message requesting the aircraft carry out a search over the lakes and look for a small aircraft that had gone missing. The passengers were summoned to the flight deck and given binoculars. The pilot said: 'Look out for a seaplane or any wreckage.'

I didn't realise that there were thousands of lakes and islands in Canada. Many people are aware of the Great Lakes but not all the others. Some Canadians have holiday homes on these islands and many have their own aircraft to take then there. We understood that the pilot of the stricken aircraft had got lost. As the fuel on the Hercules began getting low the captain radioed air traffic control and informed them that we could no longer carry on with the search. We broke off and turned back to Trentham only to find that there was no missing plane.

The pilot had expressed an intention to fly but failed to log a flight plan. He and the aircraft were in a local hanger. It took quite a few of us to stop our pilot going over and levelling the chap.

At the air base I was taken to the officers' mess where I received a warm welcome and was given a bed for the night. I phoned Colin in Toronto which was about three hundred and fifty miles away. He arrived the following morning and I drove with him to the village of Angus which is about sixty miles north of Toronto. I had not seen Colin since 1970 when he had returned for our father's funeral in Swansea. It was good to see my nieces Angela and Alison for the first time in many years, and my nephew, Steven, for the very first time.

Over the weekend we visited the spectacular Niagara Falls and Colin showed me around Toronto. It was a lovely time and over all too quickly. I had to return to the ship which by this time had sailed from Bermuda and was now in the naval base at Norfolk, Virginia.

Colin drove me to Toronto International Airport and I bought a ticket to Norfolk International Airport, Virginia, USA. I was told I'd be met there. I travelled in uniform and had my passport and ID card with me. I went through the customs checks in Toronto and arrived in New York for a connecting flight.

All American airports have a military desk and I wandered over and had a chat with the sailor on reception. I couldn't have been made more welcome. There was some confusion because I was showing no gold braid. He asked what my rank was and I explained that chaplains in the Royal Navy do not have rank. Having agreed with him that this was a good idea, I was offered their kind hospitality which was a private bar for military personnel. I had unlimited coffee and doughnuts and read the papers while I waited. I'm sure the sailor would have liked to have talked more, but he had to get back to his duties. Later on, he came back and escorted me to the departure gate. Sadly, I cannot remember his name, but I do remember his kindness.

We had an uneventful flight down to Norfolk and I was met by a midshipman who drove me to the ship. On the way to the naval base I asked him whether my Canadian weekend had been regarded with disdain and he said, 'Yes, it has'.

I got back to the ship, went to my cabin and changed, and then went down to the wardroom determined to face any unpleasantness head on. It was coffee time and most officers were gathered there. I addressed them all and said: 'Look, I'm sorry. I didn't mean to cause any upset, but it was a great opportunity and I haven't seen my brother in years. I just had to grab the chance when it came along. I apologise if you thought that I was taking advantage. Which one of you would have refused the chance?' After a while they could all see the sense in what I was saying and gradually came round.

Norfolk, Virginia is a very large city and the naval base is seventeen miles long. It was crammed full of ships and we were just a small part of it; nevertheless, we were treated to the usual generous American hospitality. We were there on 4 July, Independence Day, and our

American cousins invited the entire squadron to this great holiday celebration which comprised barbecues, games, beer pavilions and all the fun of the fair. We made a banner which proclaimed 'You owe us 200 years back taxes'. It was all taken in good part and humorous comments flew back and forth. It was great fun and broke down any barriers there might have been.

As usual, they were lavish in their hospitality. I have to say that in all the time I've been to United States, including a number of visits to the Eastern Seaboard, I've received nothing but courtesy, generosity and friendship. We were taken out to nightclubs, restaurants and bars. There were sporting events between our ships and our hosts' ships during the three-week maintenance period that we spent in Norfolk. But it wasn't all 'beer and skittles'. There was work to be done as well. Maintenance teams had come over from the UK to help and advise in *Ariadne's* mini refit. That was one issue to be dealt with – and soon we had others of a domestic nature to deal with.

Chapter Eleven

An Introduction to Uncle Sam

One evening during our stay at Norfolk an officer was exceptionally rude to me in front of the duty watch and we had a 'frank exchange of views' about his attitude in private. A week later he stumbled into my cabin and burst into tears. I closed the door and said, 'What's the matter?' It all came tumbling out. It seems that he and another officer, his 'oppo', had met two girls, but he had been unable to do the business. He had erectile dysfunction and the woman had laughed at him. This was symptomatic because he'd just gone through a difficult divorce and the effects of it were still weighing him down.

I was more than a little concerned about him. I spoke to one of my American colleagues and he said, 'Talk to the psychiatrists.' I didn't even know the Americans had them, but they did, and I phoned the medical centre and spoke to one of the psychiatrists. He was due to travel to Guantanamo Bay with his family for a week's leave. Apparently, the American Navy had a holiday resort there. He agreed to delay the start of his holiday in order to help the officer which I thought was remarkably kind. On Saturday morning I accompanied Chris to the medical centre and it was very discreet. Chris was asked if he wanted me to sit in on the interview and he declined. I stayed outside while the psychiatrist examined him. After about an hour the consultation was over and Chris came out. The psychiatrist and I went for a walk. He said: 'You've got one very sick man on your hands. He is in a very, very fragile state. He could explode or do something silly at the drop of a hat.'

I asked: 'How do we cope with the situation?'

He said: 'It's like taking the lid off a kettle. That's what you need to do for the remainder of the time that he is with you. He'll need help until you get back to the UK.' He added: 'I'll write a letter for your psychiatrists over there explaining my views.'

The letter was duly drafted and I later sent it off to a friend of mine, Morgan O'Connell, with whom I had had dealings on a number of occasions. I thanked the American psychiatrist profusely for his help and we headed back to the ship. I could only hint at Chris's problems to a few of the officers and we shielded and protected him for the rest of the deployment. Later, back in the UK, Chris was treated and became a much better man for it. He left the navy and got married again and the last I heard he was very happy.

The problem with three-week maintenance periods is that people have extended opportunities to spend time ashore. Leave is granted from 1600 to 0800 the following morning for those over the age of eighteen. Instead of coming back to the ship late in the evening, they had permission to stay ashore as long as they returned for work at the right time the next morning. The problem with this is that 'liaisons' can be created. A weapons electrical officer came to me one day and asked if I would have a word with one of his chief petty officers who had been coming in late in the mornings. During a stand easy

I had a quiet word with him: 'Enjoy yourself ashore?'

He replied, 'Do you have five minutes?'

I nodded: 'Yes.'

The flight deck wasn't in use and we went for a walk there.

'I'm going to leave the navy.'

'Why?'

'I've met this woman and she's the light of my life.'

I was aghast: 'Look Dave, I'm not here to judge you or condemn you, but you have a wife and three children at home who love you'.

'I know. It's terrible for them and selfish of me, but I love her.'

The woman concerned had been a guest that he'd met at a party in the chief's mess and it had gone further. She was a police officer and the ship was in contact with the local police department frequently. I left a message asking her to contact me. She duly did so and we met up for coffee in one of the many coffee shops dotted around the base. I believed Dave was making a big mistake which he would later regret but needed to hear her point of view. I sat across the table from this very attractive woman who told me that she too was concerned about Dave.

She said: 'I think he's a lovely man and I think the world of him, but I have no intention of getting married and I most certainly didn't want to break up his marriage. I had no idea that he felt so strongly about me. I'll try to let him down gently before it goes any further.'

That's exactly what she did. A few days later he returned to the ship in a sombre mood and was very morose for a few weeks. I'd taken the precaution of having a word with the president of the mess who knew about what had happened and was concerned about him as were his messmates. Gradually, bit by bit, with their help, he recovered his character and style and by the time we reached Miami he was back to normal.

Our maintenance period was also marked by a mysterious gift that came my way. I returned to the ship from visiting the chaplaincy centre one day and found a Japanese 'head' on my desk. It was not a real head, I hasten to add. It was the head of a Samurai warrior made from hessian and surrounded in a glossy material and filled with sawdust. It was simply a gift; it seems the Japanese make gifts that do not have any monetary value but are symbols of respect. I had no idea where it had come from or why I was so honoured. Accompanying the 'head' was a note and a newspaper cutting.

The first lieutenant, Charles Freeman, appeared behind me and demanded: 'Where's that from?' He didn't like the Japanese for some reason.

I shook my head. 'I've no idea.'

I went to the duty watch and they told me a Japanese gentleman had come on board asking for me. The guys had called one of the stewards who took the gifts from the Japanese man and placed them in my cabin. There was a significant story behind all this. It transpired that many years ago, two female childhood friends in the UK had both got married. One couple had moved to Norfolk, Virginia, while the other couple had stayed at home. The women remained in close contact over the years. Eventually both husbands died and the woman in Norfolk suggested that her friend come and live in America with her.

She explained to her friend in the UK: 'We're both widows, so why don't you come and live with me?'

And that is what happened. Neither had children, so

they were free agents. The only stipulation the lady moving from the UK made before moving was that when she died, she wanted to be buried at home in Britain, or to be precise, just off the coast at sea. The years rolled by and she did die and her friend, who was not in the best of health herself, had her cremated. The remains were kept in an urn on a sideboard.

As the surviving friend became increasingly unwell, she pondered the promise she had made, and then read in the local newspaper that *Ariadne* and the NATO squadron were in Norfolk, Virginia. She asked her neighbour, who was Japanese, if he could contact the ship. He did so by coming on board and leaving the newspaper cutting, the message and the gift. The upshot was that he later brought the urn to the ship and I received it from him, having obtained the captain's permission. I must be one of the few naval chaplains ever to have 'a woman' in his cabin for any length of time because I placed the urn on top of my wardrobe where it remained for six weeks. As soon as we entered UK waters off Cornwall the ship stopped and her remains were committed to the deep where she now rests in peace.

Modern sailors are just as superstitious as their forebears. For those six weeks there was a great reluctance on the part of quite a few of the men to enter my cabin. In many cases, the educational courses and interviews had to be carried out in an empty compartment elsewhere.

One morning I was sitting in my cabin in *Ariadne* and looking through lists of applications for courses when the curtain was pulled aside and in stumbled a chief petty officer in civilian dress whose surname was Thomas. He sat down and burst into tears. I got up and closed the door, let him cry a little bit and then said, 'Whatever is the matter?'

He shook his head: 'My mother's seriously ill back home.'

She had been unwell for some time and was deteriorating fast. Sometime earlier, he had been to see his head of department, the engineering officer, who might have been a good marine officer but knew nothing about the welfare side of the navy.

The engineering officer had told him: 'Don't worry about it, if your mother's ill, I'll ensure you get home'.

That comment allayed his fears. He didn't worry about the problem of returning home and phoned his wife at every port to receive updates on his mother's condition. His intention was to go to his head of department and ask for a warrant to go home when it was necessary – as had been intimated to him. Latterly, in Norfolk, he had been phoning home regularly from the Post Exchange, known as PX – the US Navy's equivalent of the NAFFI only better. On the morning we were due to sail, he was told that his mother had deteriorated further and he should return home urgently. A distressed Thomas had gone to his head of department and explained that his mother's health was going downhill.

The engineering officer went to the captain and said: 'Thomas needs to go home. His mother is seriously ill and she hasn't got long left.'

The captain said, 'No.'

'But I told him that he could go.'

'Well, you shouldn't have. I can't release men on the say-so of their wives at home. Has he or she been in touch with Naval Personnel Family Services?'

The marine engineering officer said that he didn't know and the captain pointed out that without a signal verifying the situation from NPFS he could not let him go. NPFS are the Royal Navy's social workers and to be fair they would bend over backwards to help in any situation, but if you're not consulted about a situation, you can't help. Not expecting a problem Thomas had got changed to prepare for the trip home. It was a bitter blow when the officer told him the news that the captain had said no. One of his oppos advised him to talk to me, hence his appearance in my cabin. By this time, we had sailed from the naval base and Norfolk, Virginia was a disappearing smudge in the distance.

Wagstaff said, 'Can you help Bish?'

I took a deep breath. 'I'll try.'

I went up to the bridge and waited until the captain had a moment and then I asked about Chief Petty Officer Thomas.

The captain bellowed: 'Thomas? Thomas? Everybody's going on about bloody Thomas. What am I supposed to do? I can't let him go if NPFS haven't verified the situation.'

I pointed out that a promise had been made by a senior officer that he would be released. I said: 'If he's prepared to pay his own fare and the ship can manage without him will he be allowed to go?'

'How am I supposed to get him ashore now that we've sailed?' demanded the captain.

'Can't we launch the Wasp and fly him back to Oceana? He could catch a flight home from there.'

'It's outside the range of the Wasp. We are about one hundred and fifty miles off Oceana. There's nothing that can be done.'

I thanked the captain for his time and went up onto the bridge and saw the Officer the Watch who was a friend of mine called Paul Nuth.

I asked: 'How far off Oceana are we?'

He took the dividers to the chart and said: 'About seventy-five miles.'

I said: 'That should be well within range of the Wasp?'

'Yup.'

The captain had been more than economical with the truth. As I said earlier, I was to cross swords with him on a few occasions and this was one of them. I was furious. I don't like being treated like an idiot. We had a Canadian officer sailing with us on exchange and he suggested: 'Call *HMCS Ottawa*. Maybe they can help. If your captain says we are out of range, you can't call him a liar to his face, so go around him. We have a Sea King on board *Ottawa*.'

The Sea King was a bigger helicopter than a Wasp with a much greater range.

I left the bridge and went down to the main communication office and asked the petty officer on watch if I could put a ship to ship call through to a friend of mine on board the *Ottawa*. Mike Crighton served there as the flight observer. When Mike came on, I explained the problem and asked if *Ottawa* could help.

'Give me five minutes,' he said, and I waited. Sure enough within five minutes he was back and it was all arranged. Mike said: 'We could pick up Thomas and fly him back in no time.'

Now my task was to 'fix' the captain. I went to his cabin and outlined the plan and he said: 'Do as you wish; I'll be glad to see the back of the man.'

It wasn't a pleasant comment, but I had got what I wanted.

I went to the communication office and made a call to *Ottawa* and our plan swung into action. I raced down to

Thomas and said: 'Get your passport, your cheque book and your kit together, the Canadians are flying you back.'

He was soon on the flight deck and within minutes was being winched up into the Sea King. The Canadians flew him into Oceana and dropped him on the apron outside the main terminal. He caught the next flight home and was in time to see his mother before she died.

I learned an important lesson from the experience. I believed that the navy must always try to help people if they have a problem, even if it means they pay their own way home but understood it was best for people to inform NPFS that they have a problem before they deploy. I think that helping men and women in times of trouble maintains their loyalty and trust. The attitude of the captain would have achieved the reverse – causing resentment, a loss of loyalty and more people wanting to leave the service. Chief Petty Officer Wagstaff rejoined us in Fort Lauderdale.

We sailed from Norfolk Virginia on 16 July and were bound for Charleston, South Carolina. We were due to arrive on 20 July. The passage to Charleston was uneventful. Officer of the watch manoeuvres were carried out and the general work patterns were re-established on board ship. Training in a multinational NATO squadron continued.

We arrived in Charleston and I agreed to act as second liaison officer. Liaison work is always busy and in a small ship with only a handful of officers it can mean some people doing a lot jobs and that's not fair; so I said 'if I can help I will'. Paul Nuth was the liaison officer and we worked together to make our visit successful in social terms and other respects too. Preparatory work had been done with the civic and naval people in Charleston prior to our arrival. Charleston is a major port and one of historic significance. The American Civil War began there in 1861 with the bombardment of Fort Sumter by the South Carolina militia.

On arrival we received a warm welcome. Paul and I went into a huddle with our hosts to look at the invitations that have been extended to us; not just the wardroom but to all the messes. Sporting arrangements had been made even though we were only going to be there for a limited time. We were due to sail just three days later. There was an awful lot to be crammed in if we were to fulfil all the invitations and not cause disappointment.

One of the courtesies of the Charleston population was 'Dial a Sailor': this was when local families offered hospitality to sailors of whatever rank. The local press published the telephone numbers of the ships, and families phoned up and offered to entertain one or more sailors for the day or for the duration of the visit. Because we were a multinational force there were people in Charlestown who were of British, Portuguese and Dutch origin, or whatever, and they would phone in and take the sailors away. We were a bit apprehensive at first, but it worked very well.

On Saturday afternoon I received a phone call from a lady who said that she and her husband would like to entertain four sailors for supper.

I said: 'I'm very sorry, but there's no one here. They've all gone.'

She was very persistent and said, 'You are there.'

'Yes, we are.'

'Can't you come?'

Paul looked at me and I at him, and he shrugged and I

said: 'Yes, thank you. Two of us can certainly take up your offer, possibly three'.

Our host said she would collect us at 1800. Our third colleague was the supply officer Adrian Munns. He agreed to join us and we were collected by this lady and taken to her lovely home and entertained to drinks and a meal. Her name was Mrs Bebe and her husband was a retired lieutenant colonel in the USAF. He was the archetype of a particular American character – an overweight southerner with a large cigar who spoke like Rooster Cogburn. That weekend, far away in Iran, the American embassy had been stormed by militarised Iranian students and fifty-two hostages held. It caused quite a shock in America. Colonel Bebe was all for 'Nuking them Iranian bastards'.

Adrian Munns gently pointed out that Britain was a bit closer to Iran than the USA and if people were going to throw nuclear weapons around, we were more likely to be polluted than America. He was promptly accused of being a 'Pinko'. It was a lively, fascinating evening. We drank mint juleps and sat on the back porch and so on. They were very kind and the hospitality was lavish, but we were miles apart in our attitude to world affairs.

On the Sunday morning we went to the Parish Church of St. Philips. It was interesting to observe the Americans when they went to church; they went in their best clothes because to them Sunday was a family day. First, they went to church and then they visited their parents' home for lunch. It was very much like Britain in the 1950s. St. Philips was a lovely Anglican church and we were made very welcome. If they had known we were going to be there, I would have been invited to preach, but I was more than happy to sit in the congregation, receive the sacrament and simply observe.

That evening Paul Nuth and I, our duties done, thought that since we were in the Deep South we would like to visit a traditional Dixieland jazz club. We had arranged for a bus to take some of the crew to such a venue and we jumped on the bus and went too. It was very good 'trad' jazz. I don't know why, but we got caught up in conversation and missed the bus going back. We thought we'd get a taxi from downtown Charleston but because the area was deemed 'historic' there were no taxis and we decided to walk back to the dockyard. It wasn't far and it was a balmy evening. As we were walking down a slight hill, not far from the dockyard gates, there were half a dozen black guys sitting on the wall on the opposite side of the road. When they saw us coming down the hill they got off the wall and crossed to our side of the road.

I said to Paul: 'I think we might have trouble coming our way.'

Paul said: 'I think you're right. What do you think we should do?'

'We have three choices. We can turn around and go back, but they'd probably chase us. We can just laugh it out, but what we should do is pray.'

I wasn't being flippant, I meant it, but as a precaution I put my ID card in one of my socks and my roll of dollar bills in the other. We were getting very apprehensive as these guys were getting closer and with that a taxi pulled up because the traffic lights near us were on red. The taxi was empty, so we opened the door and jumped in.

The taxi driver said: 'I'm not allowed to take a fare off the street.'

I said: 'My friend, I don't care, we're not getting out. See those guys in front of us? They mean business, so please take us to our ship and we'll double the fare.'

Fortunately, he did, and when we got back on board we had a drink to settle our nerves. We looked on it as a bit of an adventure; but I think if those guys had caught up with us it would not have been much fun because they saw us as fair game.

We sailed the following morning after a relatively uneventful visit. Nobody ended up in hospital and everybody was back on board on time, so we congratulated ourselves on a very successful stop-off and set sail for our next destination. Our next port of call was further south in Mayport. We were due to arrive there on 27 July and on the way we carried out exercises and manoeuvres within the squadron. The crew were given the opportunity to cross decks to other ships and see how other navies operated and what there living conditions were like.

We arrived in Mayport on schedule and the usual cocktail party took place. We were also visited by friends we had made during our stay in Norfolk. A few days earlier, while we were in Norfolk, we had booked a trip to Disneyworld which was only about a hundred and fifty miles south of Mayport. We couldn't wait for the cocktail party to end so we could have a quick change of clothes, grab our pre-packed bags and race down the gangway to the cars. It was so exciting; we felt like kids let loose.

We were only able to stay out for one night which was spent in Orlando where we had booked several rooms in a cheap motel. That evening we went to explore the delights of Orlando which were quite amazing. Rosie O'Grady's Good Time Emporium was quite a find, a restaurant and music club that was a big part of Orlando night life, and there we settled. There were bands of all sorts, playing different styles of popular music ranging from rock and roll to the polka. There were such long bars that if you ordered a drink, they would slide the glass of foaming beer along the bar, just like in the movies. We had a meal there and wore polystyrene bowlers and boater hats. It was such a fun place and we totally enjoyed the experience.

We then retired to our motel rooms because we had an early start the next morning. Since we only had a single day at Disneyworld, we decided to make the most of it and arrived before the entertainment park had even opened. The car parks were enormous and each one had the name of a Disney character. Even though 'The Magic Kingdom' wasn't yet open, the car park attendants were on site and showed us where to go.

An attendant told us: 'Remember which car park you are in. People regularly forget and there'll be fifty thousand people here today. If you forget it will take all evening to find your car'.

The name of the car park was burned into my brain so much that I can remember it to this day: we were parked in Mini 2. All day we kept asking each other, 'Which car park are we in?'

Back came the answer, 'Mini 2.'

We went to the entrance, paid our tickets, and went into this vast area of entertainment: things like a 'Pirates of the Caribbean' which was phenomenal
'Magic Mountain', and so many more, while all the Disney characters buzzed around us. The weather was glorious and we saw so much that by the end of the afternoon we were wilting.

All good things come to an end and we had to drive back to Mayport. There was a slight delay in our departure because one brave soul had to dive into the sweltering car to switch on the engine and the air conditioning.

When we got back to the ship there was sad farewells on the jetty as our friends had to return to Norfolk. We were due to sail the following morning. We only had three days in Mayport and two days were taken up with leave, so the remaining day was 'in house' catching up with the post and so on. My mail included lots of acknowledgements to applications for courses I had sent off. Some course leaders wanted more information from the guys and on passage to Fort Lauderdale I was busy chasing applicants and getting further information from them to send off when we next docked.

I also did a stint on second officer of the watch duties. You get to know the other watch keepers reasonably well by talking to them and listening to the banter. There's a saying in the navy: 'All debts are cancelled with the first turn of the screw'. It means that all debts ashore can be cancelled with the first turn of the ship's screw, but that's not always the case.

A young sailor who shared the watch with me had met and fallen in love – or lust – with a young girl in a nightclub in Mayport. She was a single parent with a little girl, so the sailor was manna from heaven as far as she was concerned. I tried to dissuade him from getting involved and said, 'You know nothing about her.'

But he was adamant he was going to marry her and said she was flying over to the UK on, 'A big silver bird.'

Despite being told by a number of people that this was a bad idea he was determined to marry her. His mood changed markedly when we arrived in Fort Lauderdale because he received a letter and a photograph from the girl. The image showed love bites on her neck which he hadn't given her and showed she been out on the town with someone else. He was advised to write to her and call the whole thing off. This he did, but imagine his consternation when we later arrived back in Devonport and he saw his parents waving to him from the jetty and the girl standing next to them. Either she had not received his letter or she had chosen to ignore it. He was a very unhappy sailor.

He came to see me in a state of confusion and I said: 'The only thing that you can do is sit down with her and be honest. Tell her that she can no longer stay with your parents and that she has to go home.' He followed my advice and paid her fare home. It was a salutary lesson: having a girl in every port in the age of easy air travel sometimes has repercussions.

As we approached Fort Lauderdale, I spotted a pelican sitting comfortably on a large buoy which had a flashing light on it marking the channel. It was the first time I'd seen a pelican and was another one of those magical moments I experienced thanks to being at sea in the Royal Navy.

We arrived in Fort Lauderdale for the squadron visit on 1 August. It was a chance for us all to take stock of the things that had been accomplished – what we had learnt as a squadron, as a ship and me as a chaplain. Our visit to Fort Lauderdale was due to end on 5 August as would our membership of STANAVFORLANT. *Ariadne* had been with the squadron for a year, a long time, and she was the longest serving ship in the squadron. Many friendships had been forged between people on the different ships, but it was time to say farewell. As with all things, nothing lasts forever and all good things come to an end. Most of *Ariadne's* ship's company were looking forward to returning home to friends and family as they had been away for such a long time. As soon as we were far out to sea, the other ships formed line astern and very slowly *Ariadne* steamed past them in the opposite direction. Each ship gave us three cheers and elevated their fire hoses and turned them on full blast. Simultaneously, all the sirens were sounding. It was an emotional moment.

As we journeyed homewards, I knuckled down to my expanded set of duties. My role as 'education officer' was time-consuming but rewarding. There were numerous courses that I was able to provide for officers and ratings. Some wanted an extra qualification because they planned to apply for premature voluntary release or because they wanted to advance in the navy. Passing NAMET, for example, enabled a number of sailors to achieve the next rank, be it able rate, leading hand or petty officer. The courses that I was able to obtain for those seeking voluntary release ranged from bricklaying and carpentry to one of the more popular ones, public service vehicle licence which was required for driving large lorries or buses. The most expensive course I applied for was for an officer who wanted to go into the television industry. I contacted ITV and they provided a course in TV production for him. It looked a very comprehensive, fulfilling course and there was an extremely good opportunity for permanent employment at the end of it. Months later I discovered that he hadn't turned up for the course. It made me angry and frustrated when an opportunity was provided for someone and they couldn't be bothered to attend.

Our passage home involved sailing north to refuel in Bermuda and we arrived there on 7 August and sailed on the next day. Our passage was across the Atlantic to the

Azores and then up through the Bay of Biscay and home. It was an uneventful passage.

At that time, I rarely took lunch. Instead, I spend the time taking my 'click- click' bed up onto roof of the bridge and did some sunbathing and listened to my favourite tape recordings. On one occasion I felt the ship heel underneath me and got up to see what it was. In the distance I could see a small white island. Intrigued, I kept watching, and when the ship got closer, it turned out to be a Beluga whale, or the remains of one, which was being attacked and eaten by sharks. Needless to say, we did not pipe 'hands to bathe'.

We arrived in the Azores on 13 August and sailed that afternoon having taken on fuel and received mail. It was our last mail delivery of the voyage and my post contained a lot of course dates and results for those who had either applied or had taken exams. The next few days were spent distributing the information to the respective students.

As we sailed north, the weather became atrocious with heavy seas and the ship rolled around like a drunken sow. As we entered the Bay of Biscay a contact was seen on the radar and we diverted to search for it. We discovered a Russian submarine wallowing on the surface. *Ariadne* circled her. Sometimes she was above us and sometimes below us, such were the horrendous weather conditions. To remain upright we clung on to whatever hand holds were available. We tried every available means to raise the submarine. She was clearly in trouble because submarines don't surface in heavy weather much less hang around on the surface. She must have been waiting for a tug or some form of rescue craft. We were completely ignored, so we had no choice but to bid her farewell and carry on our way. I have no idea what happened to her.

Coming out of the Bay of Biscay the weather was still bad and we received a signal from Northwood, the operations headquarters of the navy, to divert to the west coast to stand by for survivors of the ill-fated 1979 Fastnet race. It was a competition held every two years from the Isle of Wight to Fastnet Rock, the most southerly point of Ireland, and then back to Plymouth via the Scilly Isles. The competitors were caught in a fierce storm with mountainous seas and it led to serious loss of life. Fifteen sailors and four rescuers died. Five boats sank and seventy-five flipped over. It led to one of the largest rescue operations in modern maritime history.

Ariadne sent a message back to Northwood explaining that if we were to stand by for survivors, we needed an oiler to come out and refuel us. In the event, we were ordered to return to Devonport and *Broadsword* was sent out instead. The international rescue effort for the Fastnet sailors involved ships and air sea rescue services from the UK, Ireland and France. The former Prime Minister, Edward Heath, captaining his yacht Morning Cloud, was a competitor. At one stage he and his crew were reported missing. Later he was located and towed to safety.

We made our way back up the English Channel. One Royal Navy ship board practice that I gather has now been discontinued was 'Up Channel Night'. It was 'party time' the night before reaching home port for a ship returning after a long deployment. *Ariadne's* individual mess decks created their own entertainment. Apart from the watch keepers, copious quantities of alcohol were consumed. I was invited down to one of the mess decks; I can't remember which one. Two or three messes had assembled as one. There were sailors hanging off bunks and a good singsong was in progress. I had been trying, unsuccessfully, to buy a Confederate flag and during a lull in proceedings, with great solemnity, I was presented with one by a sailor. I don't know how they knew I wanted the flag, but I was deeply touched by the gesture and thanked them all profusely.

I had earned my pennies on the trip and a number of sailors had been helped by my ministrations. My head the following morning was not as clear as it should have been and that was illustrated by what I did on arrival. When we were alongside and the gangway had gone down, I crossed it and went to the wardroom in *HMS Drake* to get the keys of my cabin from the hall steward. I went to my cabin, got the keys to my garage and drove my car down to the ship, so I could put my gear in the boot. We hadn't cleared customs so what I had done was illegal. In an unguarded moment in the wardroom a little later, I mentioned my car was on the jetty.

I said: 'Does anybody want a lift?'

The captain ears pricked up and he wanted to know how come my car was on the jetty when we hadn't cleared customs. Quick as a flash the first lieutenant Charles Freeman said: 'I gave the chaplain permission to go because he needed to get into Plymouth quickly to see someone who leaving. I hope that was alright?'

The captain glowered and said, 'Yes of course it is.'

Charles had saved my bacon and I was very grateful to him; it could have been quite awkward given my relationship with the captain. Having cleared customs, I gathered up my possessions, put them in the car and took my leave of the crewmates who had become my friends. Most I would never meet again, but it been a very interesting three months and I had enjoyed the whole experience. It was good to be home and I was looking forward to my brief leave before joining my next ship which was to be *HMS Berwick* again.

Leave is always a welcome and necessary break from the sea and this one was no exception. We visited friends and family and the weather that August was glorious. We spent a lot of time on the Gower beaches especially Caswell where we almost took up residence.

A shocking event took place in Ireland that month. It was an incident that caused outrage around the world. On 27 August, Lord Louis Mountbatten was assassinated. His yacht was blown up off the coast of Mullaghmore. He and three other people died. I remember we were unpacking all our kit from a day on the beach when the news came through on the television that he had been assassinated.

I met Lord Louis on two occasions, both of them at Amport when he came to talk at our chaplains' conference. He was not the nicest of men and I cannot say that I liked him but for all that, it was sad that someone who had served the country so courageously during the Second World War should have his life ended in such a despicable way. I may not have liked him, but he deserved a better fate than that.

Leave was over all too soon and I returned to my cabin in the wardroom at *HMS Drake*. A number of ships in the squadron were beginning to go into refit, so I whiled away my days visiting them in their refit conditions, having lunch with those on board, and dropping in on the various departments and talking to the sailors. There were requests for baptisms which meant that if they lived in Plymouth I would visit families in their homes which was always a pleasure. It was also time to catch up with what was happening in the chaplains' branch. The current Chaplain of the Fleet, Basil O'Ferrall was due to retire from naval ministry after long and faithful service. It was odds on that Ray Roberts would succeed him. Ray, my friend and mentor from Lympstone days, had been appointed chaplain to *HMS Drake* and had moved into a cabin suite just along the passage from me. It meant I was able to a catch up with him and find out what was going on in the branch.

One day after breakfast he said to me: 'I've received a letter from the Chaplain of the Fleet saying that the senior Anglican chaplain of the US Navy is visiting Britain and is due to pay a visit to Plymouth. He's asked whether we will entertain him for a day. What am I going to do with him? Any ideas?'

I said: 'You could take him round the various historical sites of interest like the Hoe and tell him the story about Drake playing bowls before defeating the Armada. You could then go out to Buckland Monachorum and see Drake's Drum and then call in at The Rutland Arms which is a very nice pub and give him lunch or dinner. Maybe throw in a Devon cream tea on the way.'

Ray thought it a good schedule. 'Excellent, you can accompany us.'

I was stunned and said: 'I was only asked for suggestions; I gave you suggestions.'

'Yup, and you're going to give me your company too'.

It was a very pleasant day. The senior US Navy chaplain was one Admiral Charles 'Chuck' Kaiser, who was a very big man and a delight. He was more than happy with the informal programme we had prepared for him. On his arrival, we introduced ourselves and had coffee in the wardroom. After a tour of the dockyard, we toured Plymouth, the Hoe and went up onto Dartmoor. He viewed Dartmoor Prison and other sites before reaching the picturesque village of Buckland Monachorum, which is mentioned in the Domesday Book. We finished up at The Rutland Arms for a wonderful meal in front of a roaring fire.

All in all, 'Chuck' was thrilled with the tour we had laid on. We had given him a flavour of the West Country and throughout the day he chatted to us about the way our chaplains carried out their duties. He returned to London having learned a lot about how chaplains operate in the Royal Navy.

I got ready to join the *Berwick*. Her role was to be a Belize guard ship and that meant she would be away for Christmas. I always worked on the principle that if the ships were away for the festive season, then so was I. Before we sailed, I had long weekend leave in Swansea with Jeannetta, the children and my mother, and then returned to Devonport. I was due to join the ship on 4 November. It was my third time on board, so I knew the ship's company very well. There had been changes, but the bulk of the crew was still the same. It was good to meet them again and they welcomed me as a friend as well as their priest and it promised to be a good deployment.

Chapter Twelve

We Become Celebrities in Florida

Our deployment as a guard ship meant that we had to be within five days steaming of Belize. The reason for a guard ship was because of a longstanding territorial dispute between Guatemala and Belize. Belize was Britain's last colony on the America mainland and was not independent at the time. Our military presence also included an army battalion and RAF aircraft.

We sailed for Central America on 5 November, 1979, and I was full of anticipation for a new adventure. We refuelled in the Azores and were there for two days. We received a mail drop just before we sailed and one letter provided an unpleasant shock for the recipient.

That evening I went for a shower. Suddenly the door of the bathroom burst open and a sailor stumbled in. His face was streaked with tears. I told him to leave at once and wait for me outside my cabin. Having negotiated the ladders in flip flops, I returned to my cabin, got dressed and invited him in. His tear-stained face looked up at me and he held out a letter. It was a classic 'Dear John' missive which had arrived in the last batch of mail. No sooner had we sailed from Plymouth than his wife had sat down and written the letter. She was leaving him. She said she couldn't cope with being a naval wife and that was that. But there was more. Someone else was involved. You can imagine the distress a letter like causes a sailor, particularly when you've just set sail and can't immediately return home.

I said: 'Do you want compassionate leave? You could fly home when we get to Bermuda.'

He shook his head: 'What's the point? If she's made up her mind to go off with this other guy, there's no point.'

'Okay, we'll do what we can to help you.'

I let him talk at length about how he felt. Later that evening, with his permission, I asked the leading hand of his mess to come and see me. I explained what had happened and asked him to quietly let the rest of his mates know too because he was going to be very down for a while. I pointed out that filling him with alcohol would be a very bad idea. I said: 'Just support him and let him come to terms with his situation in his own time.'

Not long after leaving the Azores we ran into a Force 8 gale. The following Sunday was Remembrance Sunday. It's the one day you can guarantee a full turn out at church. The master at arms, Phil Shapiro, helped me organize the service. Phil was a close friend and I served with him again later; I was also to conduct his mother's funeral.

That Remembrance Day we were to have hymns sang unaccompanied, the captain would read the lesson and so on. In readiness for the service, but with great misgivings, I took my surplice to the laundry and established that a) the Chinese laundryman knew what it was, and b) to iron it without folds. He assured me that all would be well, but on my return to my cabin I found that it was starched and folded like a shirt. Since the laundry was closed and all the laundrymen were in hiding, I had no alternative but to iron it myself in the chief's mess because the wardroom didn't have an ironing board or iron. With one foot against the bulkhead, to brace myself against the roll of the ship, I had to hang onto the iron and ironing board at the same time. The chiefs thought it hilarious and eventually I saw the funny side and enjoyed a pint with them on completion of a rather awkward task.

The following morning the turbulent sea had abated slightly and the service was, as usual, scheduled for 1100. We held it on the upper deck down aft and I stood on a grating while the ship's company were gathered around. A watery sunshine – no pun intended – brightened the sky though there was a breeze. The sailors were now in tropical rig (whites) and all sported the red poppy. I was facing for'ard and the service began. I preached a sermon and as I was coming to the end, I saw a great wave rolling down the starboard waist. It flooded the after deck. The sailors were ankle deep in water, but I was safe on the grating. Undaunted, we sang the final hymn and everyone adjourned to their mess decks to dry out. The general consensus was that God had decided I was preaching too long and had sent the wave to shut me up!

We arrived in Bermuda and berthed at Ireland Island. We had a few days in Bermuda before we sailed south for other parts of the Caribbean. There had to be a handover with the ship we were relieving, *HMS Ambuscade*, commanded by Commander Mike Gretton. I can still remember the ships' crests painted on the walls of the dock, many going back to the Second World War.

Bermuda is a lovely island. The weather was beautiful and the sailors hired mopeds and raced off around the island. Having completed the handover, we sailed from

Bermuda on November 20 and arrived in Nassau two days later for a four-day visit. Traditionally, we held a cocktail party on the first evening which was always good value. There were sporting activities on the Saturday and on Sunday, and I held a service of Holy Communion on the bridge at 0800 and then we went to Nassau Cathedral for the 1100 service.

It was quite amusing really because you had a very mixed congregation and it was all a bit like Britain in the 1950s and 60s. I remember the dean, who was a native of Nassau, stopping the choir and taking magazines and chewing gum from the choirboys. It was a lovely service which I enjoyed and we had a great welcome. Sadly, only a few of our people came with me, just half a dozen or so. The weather was warm, not too hot, and the sky blue and cloudless. It was difficult to believe that we were only a few weeks away from Christmas.

One strange sight was cotton wool around the edges of the windows, replicating snow, while Christmas lights hung from the shops and along the main street. It was very much like a bit of Britain in the sunshine and we enjoyed our few days among a kind and hospitable people.

We sailed from Nassau on 26 November. Three days later our helicopter was launched as we approached Belize because it was going to be serviced at the RAF base by our engineers. The flight commander was Joe Thomas, an American on exchange from the US Navy. Joe was from New York City and a smashing guy. I got on very well with him. The RAF did a good job of looking after him.

Our time in Belize promised to be eventful because it was so different to the other places we had visited. To begin with, there was no harbour and no harbour facilities such as a jetty. We went to anchor offshore having first negotiated the reef.

Most of Belize is jungle. It has a tropical climate with wet and dry seasons. The British Army found it splendid for jungle and mountain training and survival courses. We had fourteen Royal Marines on board: a sergeant, a corporal and twelve marines. Their messdeck was known as 'The Barracks'. They were part of the ship's company and did all the usual things like chipping paint and other ship board maintenance chores. But first and foremost, they were soldiers. Belize was 'manna from heaven' as far as they were concerned.

Since I had served with 40 Commando, they felt I understood their needs. I went to see the captain and asked if they could be released for a few days to carry out jungle training and other military activities. He agreed and a short course was arranged with the help of the resident battalion. The marines disappeared into the jungle early one morning and reappeared the afternoon before we sailed. They were covered in mosquito bites, had sustained some lumps and bumps but were very pleased with themselves and I could do no wrong in their eyes.

The weather was a great change from Nassau. Instead of beautiful sunshine, low clouds marched in, the air grew humid and rain duly followed. Transport to and from the ship was provided by the Royal Corps of Transport who ran barges bringing supplies and people.

On the first night we held our traditional and always successful cocktail party. The people who came were a familiar mix of local dignitaries but with a greater number of military personnel than usual.

On Friday I went ashore because I'd been invited to a tour of the military base by the resident army chaplain

175

who was with the Royal Enniskillin Dragoon Guards. He was a really nice chap and very welcoming. I was invited to take part in the Sunday service, to which I readily agreed. While on a tour of the base I met the officer in charge of entertainment and he told me that an ENSA troop were out there. I asked him whether they would be prepared to come out to the ship, subject to the captain's approval. He went off to check and came back and said they could turn up on Sunday evening. I told him that I would confirm the arrangement later.

We also called into the sick bay and talked to the medical officer who told me that our petty officer medical assistant (POMA) had already been scrounging items that we didn't have on the ship. Our discussion with the officer was wide-ranging, and during it he informed us that a major risk for servicemen was the danger of contracting VD. It is a fact of life that young soldiers will seek out female company at every opportunity and it can be dangerous to their health. More so sailors! I was deeply concerned that our sailors should not go with local women because the local strain of VD was largely immune to antibiotics and could devastate lives. To prevent this, the army with – in my opinion – great sense, organised a brothel under the guise of a night club. With a lack of subtlety or imagination, it was called 'The Big C'. The girls were flown in from Mexico and the US, had their own rooms and were checked out medically every two weeks. If they were found to be infected, they were sent for treatment. Our POMA was fully briefed by the military's medical staff as to the dangers facing arriving sailors.

The weather had closed in and the rain was torrential. Tropical rainstorms can be brutal. On one occasion, as I climbed down the ladder from the ship into the barge for a trip to the military base, the rain hurt my hands as they clung onto the rungs of the ladder. I'd never known anything like it.

On Sunday I went up to church and preached to a small congregation. Not many people came with me, but nevertheless the opportunity was there. Afterwards the military chaplain and I went into the base mess for lunch. The bar wasn't open, but there was a large number gathered around it. In private, the chaplain confided his concerns about the level of alcohol consumption. Belize is terrific if you're an outward-bound sort of person and enjoy jungle trekking, mountaineering, underwater swimming and exercising. But that's not for everyone.

Some whiled away their time in local bars. Resident battalions and squadrons doing six-month stints found that when they returned to the UK the level of alcohol consumption remained high. Men had got so used to large amounts of alcohol at a cheap price in Belize that they carried on in the same vein on their return home. The result was that there was a rise in alcoholism with an impact on individuals and their families. My colleague and I watched the men hanging round the bar and as soon as the shutters went up, the newspapers were dropped and the drinking began. The local chaplain told me that some of these people wouldn't bother with lunch and would just drink until the bar closed. In some ways it was understandable. Home and family were a long way away and there was not much to do on the social side of life, so the bar took over.

On Tuesday night the wardroom was invited for supper in the officers' mess at the base after which it was decided that a joint run ashore would be a good idea. We piled into a variety of vehicles and went to explore Belize City and eventually ended up at 'The Big C'. I wanted to see what it was like. It was nothing like the red-light district in Antwerp. There were even local women offering themselves outside the 'night club'. I was told on the grapevine – and glad to hear – that most of our sailors had not taken the bait. The décor inside 'The Big C' was impressive, rather like an upmarket seventies disco. The men danced with the girls, propositioned them, and if the woman liked the look of an individual, she invited him back to her room. It was all very discreet. I heard that one of our people was actually paid for his services, but it was probably a boast on his part. I think some people were surprised by my attitude to all this, but I think that sociologically and, in every way, it was a wise move on the army's part to recognise the danger and deal with matters appropriately. We returned to the ship content that our sailors were not likely to have their lives ruined and were well protected. As we stood waiting for the transport back to the ship, I was amazed at the size of the rats scurrying around the jetty; they were huge.

The ENSA concert was arranged for the Sunday night, and I explained to the captain, first lieutenant, master at arms and the entire ship's company, how it was going to work. We had an awning rigged over the flight deck and the initial idea was to keep the sun off the audience. But when the time came it was actually raining hard. The ship's helicopter was at the RAF base, so we had an empty hanger available and that became the 'theatre stage'.

That evening the entertainers came out on a barge. They were allocated a cabin for changing rooms. Chairs were brought up from below and arranged under the awning. The show was due to commence at 1930 and members of the crew carried up their cans of beer, cigarettes or snacks and sat in foul weather gear underneath the awning. It leaked like a sieve. The performers were completely dry in the hanger. The gap between the awning and the front of the hanger was only four inches and the water poured down there like a waterfall. It was a surreal view, watching the performers appear like apparitions behind a cascade of water while we were hunched over our tins of beer in foul weather gear.

The show was scheduled to last about an hour and a half and it had singers, a comedian, a magician and some dancers. Despite the conditions we had a great time. Those who were there will look back on it and laugh at the durability of sailors who will put up with any conditions to be entertained.

We were due to sail from Belize on 9 December which was a Sunday. I was looking forward to holding a church service after we had sailed and cleared the reef. Belize's reef is the second largest coral reef system in the world after Australia's Great Barrier Reef and something that needs careful navigation. Our Sunday routine was knocked sideways because our captain, John Tolhurst, had gone ashore the afternoon before with the commanding officer of the resident battalion to visit one of the outlying islands and had not returned.

The problem was the volatile weather. The rain had intensified to such an extent that they couldn't get off the island at the allotted time. Technically, he was adrift, and we couldn't sail without him. Even if he had been on board, we still couldn't have sailed because of the heavy rain. We needed the help of the radar to assist us in clearing the reef and without it, it would have been dangerous to make an attempt.

I went to the operations room and saw the radar screens filled with masses of white dots which represented the rain hitting the water with incredible force. We were stuck. Which was just as well as it gave the captain time to get back to the ship. The rain eventually eased, the captain returned and we were able to pull up the 'pick' and head for open water.

A footnote to this was that our helicopter still had to rejoin the ship. Joe Thomas, the pilot, took off from the RAF base during a lull in the weather, but five minutes into the flight the rain swept in again. The windscreen wipers couldn't clear the screen and he had to land on a beach until the squall had passed. He then took off and landed on the flight deck to discover the force of the rain had taken paint off the sides of the helicopter. By then we were out into open water and on our way to our next destination which was Miami.

Having seen Miami depicted in films and TV series, we were excited to be heading there. Before our arrival, I had had an idea which later proved a tremendous success: it was for a team of runners from the ship to run across the State of Florida from Miami to the city of St Petersburg where we were to spend Christmas. St Petersburg was on the western side of Florida on the Gulf of Mexico and I thought it would be a good idea to do a charity fundraiser and boost the profile of the ship. We wanted the good people of St Petersburg to know that we were going to be in town and were anxious to become friends. I was the unofficial entertainment officer on board, so at a meeting of the ship's welfare committee I suggested a charity run and explained it would generate goodwill. The sailors might get invitations to local people's homes for

Christmas. The response from people on board was enthusiastic. After a bit of research, I discovered that there was a children's hospital in the city, so the goal was to raise funds for it.

The consulate staff thought it was a great idea and contacted the hospital and city authorities. We started to make preparations and hired a minibus, had running vests emblazoned with the ship's name on them and plotted a route and booked accommodation. Even before we had taken a step on our two hundred and sixty-seven mile marathon, our charity run had captured the imagination of St Petersburg. There were newspaper stories about us and there was coverage on TV. I even agreed to phone the local newspaper every night with a report on our progress. The ship's welfare fund agreed to pay for the minibus and I appealed for volunteers to take part in the run. There were twelve in the party under the command of one of the ship's lieutenants. I was second in command. There were three Royal Marines and the remainder of the party were sailors from different departments who were able to spare them. The plan was that when the ship sailed from Miami and headed for the Florida Keys, we would commence our run and reach St Petersburg to coincide with the ship's arrival there.

On Sunday there was a church service on board although it wasn't the best attended. Later that day, Joe Thomas and I went for a walk along the beach and were whistled at by a group of 'gay' men, all in tight, skimpy bathing costumes and glistening with suntan oil. I was sorely tempted to invite them for drinks on board and then push off, leaving them in the hands of our first lieutenant whom nobody liked. Joe, though amused at the prospect, thought it an unchristian act and I reluctantly agreed.

Another incident that sticks in my memory was that one evening some ladies were in the wardroom. Our marine engineer officer had agreed to take two of them ashore and was looking for someone to accompany them. Reluctantly, I agreed. I wasn't keen on their company especially when one of them kept calling me 'honey'. I was looking for a way out when, to my relief, we got to a bar and a party of our sailors were there. It was a very big place, but they spotted us and called out, 'Come and join us Bish'.

Their company was preferable to that of the ladies, so I said, 'Please excuse me for a moment', and went over to the lads.

After a few minutes there was a great deal of sniggering and when I turned around there was a naked lady standing there. I say 'naked' because all she had on were her shoes. She was a waitress – and this was a 'Topless, Bottomless Bar'. I'd never heard of such a place. I was stunned, so I looked at her and asked: 'Why are you working here? Let me guess, you are divorced and have children and this job is a means of support.'

Her eyes filled with tears and she nodded. I put my hand in my pocket and took out all the money I had and pressed it into her hand.

'Go home to your children,' I said. 'There are better jobs than this.'

As I made the remark a large hand gripped my shoulder and a gruff voice said: 'Hey buddy, she's here to serve drinks, okay. Are you buying or what?'

The girl swiftly disappeared and an even bigger hand closed over the barman's wrist and a Scottish voice growled: 'I wouldna like my mother working in a place like this either.'

'Yeah, of course,' said the barman. 'What'll it be?'

I didn't want to hang around for much longer. I returned to the ladies, quickly excused myself and headed for the ship. After all, I had no money. On the way back to the ship – and many times since – I reflected on the curious morality of sailors.

Earlier that same day, in the afternoon, three of our petty officers went on a shopping trip ashore and were looking in a camera shop window. One went around the corner to look at another window display and was mugged. He had his wallet, watch and ID card all stolen at knife point. He was a few feet from his friends but out of sight. It was a salutary reminder that that we needed to be alert at all times because it was after all a foreign country.

The most notable event at sea at that time came during a 'Measured Mile' exercise. We were conducting trials with the help of US Navy boffins by running the ship over a nautical mile at full speed. They would record all the relevant data. It was a boring exercise. One forenoon, the tedium was broken when the radio burst into life on the bridge.

'Warship *Berwick,* warship *Berwick,* this is Florida Coastguard, this is Florida Coastguard are you receiving me, over?'

The petty officer communicator flicked the switch and replied: 'Florida Coastguard, Florida Coastguard, this is warship *Berwick*, warship *Berwick*, over.'

This went back and forth a few times until the captain, not in the best of moods, yelled: 'For God's sake, PO, tell them to send their message.'

Back came the reply: 'Warship *Berwick,* I have a

message for you from one, Petty Officer James McKechnie. Message reads: "Do not pay the ransom I have escaped!"'

The captain was not best pleased by the 'joke' and as he passed me to leave the bridge I muttered, 'A sense of humour in all things, sir.'

He glared at me and carried on. After he'd gone, the people on the bridge collapsed in hoots of laughter. Jim McKechnie had gone ashore the night before and got 'trapped' ashore, failing to make to make it back by the time we sailed. He was an amazing character who had been promoted to petty officer and lost that rate more times than anyone could remember and was in trouble again. We were back alongside later that day, so he sheepishly came up the gangway to be arrested by the master at arms, to appear before an immediate 'captain's table', a disciplinary hearing.

I was in my cabin after supper when the phone rang. It was Jim, who had a lantern jaw and looked like Desperate Dan in the Beano comic, inviting me to the petty officers' mess for a drink. Puzzled, I went along, and when I walked into the mess, a large number of his messmates were present. He said to me with great solemnity and in broad Glaswegian: 'I have you to thank for saving my rate. If I'd lost it this time my wife would have killed me.'

I didn't like to point out to him that if his wife had found out why he'd missed the ship, he'd be a dead man anyway. It seems that my comment in passing to the captain had caused him to take a more benevolent view of McKechnie's lapse and smile about it all. At the table he told Jim: 'You have the chaplain to thank for my leniency. I'm not going to dis-rate you, but you will have no more shore leave until Christmas.'

I said to Jim: 'You really need to get a reliable watch!'

My time for the next few days was largely taken up in preparations for the run, ensuring we had enough funds in reserve to cover what we were doing. Accommodation was not a problem because there were plenty of motels en route.

On 17 December, we waved the ship off and began our run. I contacted the newspaper in St Petersburg from phone boxes at the motels to let them know our progress. We stopped at a number of resorts one of which was called Kissimmee. While we were having a meal that evening a number of men on a nearby table got up and came across to us. We thought there was going to be trouble, but they introduced themselves politely and I invited them to join us. They were interested in what we were up to and we chatted to them for a long time.

One of them said: 'Where are you from?'

'Plymouth,' we replied.

'Is that Plymouth, New England.'

'No, Plymouth old England.'

One of them said, 'I think I've heard of that.'

We looked at one another in amazement and not for the first time I realised that the average American is incredibly insular and not really aware of what's going on in the world; at least that's how it seemed at that time. I must say the American guys were friendly and kind and we shook hands at the end of the evening before going to our rooms for a much-needed night's sleep for the next day's running.

The following morning, we were up early and on our way. One thing that that we had to contend with was substandard roads. Once you get outside the major cities the roads are not that great. I was under the impression that all things American were pristine and wonderful. I had this image of smooth, wide roads, but that wasn't the case; they were just very average two-lane roads and we had to be very careful about exactly where we were running. We kept to the usual rules of running towards the traffic, but because the Americans were not used to pedestrians out in the 'sticks', let alone runners, we had the distinct impression that we were being 'hunted' by lorries that gave angry blasts on their horns. We had a Union Flag on one side of the minibus and a White Ensign on the other so our group rather stood out.

The routine was that we would drop a runner off and move on a mile and wait until he came into view then the next runner would take over. It was a relay with nobody running more than one mile at a time. It was all rather 'stop and start', but at least that way we didn't get anybody exhausted. At times we had to do some high stepping because there were snakes at the sides of the roads. I, for one, was anxious not to get bitten.

On the outskirts of St. Petersburg there's what is called, 'The Sunshine Skyway', an elevated motorway that crosses the river. There was no way round this, so we had to climb into the minibus and cross in motorised transport rather than using leg-power. We were given a police escort with lights flashing and siren wailing.

Once across The Skyway we were nearly in the port and all thirteen runners alighted from the minibus and ran as a group onto the jetty. A gaggle of television cameras and radio reporters greeted us. The ship's company had mustered on the port side and applauded us as we arrived. It was a momentous occasion for each of the runners. We had thoroughly enjoyed the run, an experience none of us would forget. The crew had sponsored us to the tune of $1,000 for the children's hospital in St Petersburg. As leader of the group, I was interviewed by the television, radio and written press. For a few brief moments we were celebrities in St Petersburg. Our secondary aim had also been achieved because nearly every sailor was invited to a home for Christmas.

The next day I and the runners went to the Children's Hospital to present the cheque. The hospital was extremely modern and boasted every possible piece of equipment. It needed our one thousand dollars like I needed a hole in head. Nevertheless, they were extremely grateful for our gift and it was used to buy toys on one of the specialist wards. We were photographed with the children and with the members of staff and some of our people got very friendly with the nurses. That was inevitable for they were 'Jolly Jack Tars' and away from home. (Jolly Jack Tar being affectionate nickname for a British seaman.)

At the cocktail party on the day of arrival, I had met a gentleman whose family owned a construction company in St. Petersburg. His name was Billy Mills and he was a multi-millionaire. Sadly, I lost track of him, but Billy was an exuberant, ebullient, noisy character, filled with goodwill toward us, and a great Anglophile to boot. Later, during the Falklands War, he raised a great deal of money for the Royal Navy. He strongly believed the Queen was more of a head of state than President of United States would ever be. I found that in the southern states of America there was a very high regard for Her Majesty the Queen and it was certainly true in the case of Billy. He was kind enough to invite me, the captain, and the captain's wife, who had flown in for the festive season, to spend Christmas at his apartment.

The day after my visit to the hospital I was called to the gangway where a clergyman was waiting. I discovered that he was the Canon Missioner of the Episcopalian Cathedral (the American version of the Church of England) in St Petersburg; not surprisingly, the cathedral was dedicated to Saint Peter. I invited him to the wardroom where we had coffee and chatted. He invited me to his home that evening and later came to pick me up. I enjoyed a very pleasant time with him and his family, and he asked whether I would like to preach at the cathedral at Midnight Mass on Christmas Eve. It was a great honour and I was so pleased to accept.

News of our charity run had reached every corner of the city and I think that's why I had received the Midnight Mass invitation. On Christmas Eve I was collected by one of the members of staff of the cathedral and taken there in good time for the midnight service which commenced at 2330. The cathedral was packed and by 'packed' I mean that not only was the cathedral full, the adjacent hall to it (which was even bigger than the cathedral) was also full. The service was relayed to the hall on loudspeakers. There were four policemen on traffic duty outside the cathedral directing cars into the car parks in the surrounding area. When was the last time you heard of four policemen being on traffic duty outside a British cathedral?

I preached and then con-celebrated with the cathedral clergy. They seemed to like what I said (or maybe they wanted some time off!) because I was asked if I would preach the following morning. I accepted the invitation and when I got back to the ship, I had to rush through my stock of sermons to see if I had anything that I could use. As it happened, I did, and I was able to present an entirely different sermon. On completion of the morning Mass, and having taken my leave of the members of the cathedral staff, I was taken back to the ship where I changed and joined my colleagues for drinks and the 'Secret Santa' game.

The 'Secret Santa' is the gifting of cheap, silly presents; it's just a fun occasion. When we'd done the original draw in Nassau the first name out of the hat was that of the first lieutenant, a miserable and tight-fisted Scot. In preparation for the game I had bought a purse within a purse within a purse – a bit like Russian dolls – and put some coins in the final purse. I got the zip soldered closed by the ship's carpenter. There was no way the final purse could be opened. When 'The Jimmy' opened his present and got to the last purse and couldn't open it, he didn't find it at all amusing. There were hoots of laughter at his reaction.

When 'Secret Santa' was over we served Christmas dinner to the sailors of the lower deck who were still on board. Then we were off to Billy's apartment for Christmas dinner. I say 'we', and by that I mean Captain John and Mrs Tolhurst and some of my colleagues from the wardroom. A number of the crew's families had come over from the UK, paying their own fares to spend Christmas in Florida. In the Tolhursts' case, John was standing down as captain of *Berwick* and was being relieved on station in Houston on 31 December by Commander Robin Fisher who was flying into Houston airport on that day. John and his wife were then going to take the chance of a holiday in the United States as soon as the handover had taken place.

Christmas lunch was the first of a number of social activities that we were able to fit in. Billy Mills' hospitality was lavish and on our last night in St Petersburg he threw an enormous party for the entire wardroom and their wives at the penthouse of the building in which he lived. The penthouse was an enormous conference and meeting area and we had the most wonderful food and unlimited drinks.

All good things come to an end. and We sailed from St. Petersburg on 28 December and headed into the Gulf of Mexico. We were to transit the Houston canal which is a water way of about fifty miles, stretching inland from the Gulf of Mexico to the turning basin at Houston itself.

Houston is a major city in the state of Texas and we looked forward to our time in The Lone Star State. The only annoying thing for the ship's company was that they would have to be in 'Procedure Alpha' for the entire run up the canal which meant that they had to be in their best No1 uniforms and be at attention or stand at ease depending on what or who we were passing. It was all about showing respect.

It was very cold as we headed into the canal. It's a common idea that the Gulf of Mexico is warm and it is, but sometimes in the course of a year temperatures can drop and that's what had happened on this occasion. Standing on the upper deck during 'Procedure Alpha' could be very boring even when the weather was good, but in cold weather it was a lot worse.

To alleviate the tedium, I was tasked with keeping the ship's company informed of what we were passing and its history; for example, the *USS Texas*, a First World War battleship for which a special dock had been built. As we passed the *Texas*, the ship's company was called to 'attention' and the White Ensign dipped in respect. I was running to and fro, from one bridge wing to the other, spotting landmarks and points of interest and describing them in as interesting a way as possible.

I had done my homework before we entered the canal while talking to Billy Mills and spending some time scrutinising maps showing places to highlight. I had a well-prepared script and even though I was running back and forth, from one side to the other, and using microphones from the bridge wings, I was freezing. It was ten times worse for the sailors.

Billy had been invited by John Tolhurst to accompany us across the Gulf of Mexico and up the canal and he accepted with alacrity. The captain couldn't look after Billy all the time because he had a ship to run, so I was asked to host him for a lot of the time which I did with pleasure. We became firm friends.

Berwick arrived in Houston on Saturday, 29 December, and on the 30th church services were held on board. They weren't terribly well attended but Billy came together with the captain and we had an interesting discussion in the wardroom afterwards.

John Tolhurst's time as captain was coming to an end. His successor, Commander Robin Fisher, had booked into a hotel in the city and on New Year's Eve, Gordon Burns, one of the officers, and I drove to the hotel to collect him and his luggage and escort him to the ship. The handover was completed and John Tolhurst and Billy Mills left the ship to return to St. Petersburg where John was to have the holiday with his wife.

Commander Fisher settled in and invited me to give him a brief on how I found the ship's company. He was a devout man and valued chaplains. Sadly, I was to leave the ship very soon myself, so regrettably I did not serve with him for very long. New Year's Eve was spent on board and earlier the ship's company had asked for permission to set off fireworks at midnight. They were given the green light for a display which lit up the night sky. The ship's bell was rung thirteen times (a naval tradition) and the captain joined us in the wardroom for drinks. What we didn't know was that a complaint was winging our way from the port authorities because apparently you had to ask for permission to set off fireworks in the port area. We knew nothing of that. Apologies were sent and accepted and you can't really undo fireworks when they've gone off.

Chapter Thirteen

A Farewell to the Royal Navy?

The great state of Texas provided an entertaining start to 1980. I was due to fly home on 7 January, so I had the best part of a week in Houston. The consulate staff were very kind and showed us around. There were a number of functions on board where we met people who invited us to different events including a rodeo. The Americans insisted that the sailors should go in rig which didn't please them all, but we went anyway and it was good fun.

Britain could fit into Texas eight times over and it never ceased to amaze me how far people would travel for entertainment. The rodeo was about seventy-five miles from Houston, but that didn't seem to bother our hosts. It was a huge venue with several thousand people present. We watched bronco busting and steer riding and all the things you see in western films. At one point an announcement was made that Royal Navy sailors were in the auditorium and we were invited to take part in catching a calf by roping it with lassos. The lads took part and it was a hoot; the audience gave them rousing applause. On the way to the rodeo, we were stopped for a long time by a 'grain train' which was the best part of a mile long, trundling along the tracks, transporting the grain to the Houston canal and an onward destination.

Another sporting fixture that we attended was an American football game at the Houston Astrodome, an enormous stadium which had a scoreboard costing $1 million. It was a fabulous venue. The match was the US College Final, but I found American football boring. It went on too long. There were constant changes of players depending on whether they were defending or attacking.

On a later occasion in Miami, I and a midshipman called Peter Morgan, another Welshman, were given tickets to watch the Miami Dolphins play the New York Jets. It took place on a gorgeous day under a brilliant sun and it was a great occasion. Peter was a lovely man who later distinguished himself during the Falklands Campaign. He was awarded the DSO in the campaign for saving the ship that he was serving in. He also helped to dislodge a bomb that had struck *Argonaut*, leading to her long refit (see below).

The reason that I was flying home on 7 January was because I had been invited to travel to Gibraltar to recommission *HMS Apollo*. *Apollo* had been in refit in Gibraltar for two years and *HMS Ariadne* was going in for a refit. The ship's company of *Ariadne* was to crossover to *Apollo* and bring her out as *Ariadne* went into dry dock. As I explained earlier, I got to know *Ariadne's* ship's company very well indeed and as a result they asked if I could come and commission the ship. It wouldn't happen today, a chaplain being flown across the world just to commission a ship, but it did then.

I caught a flight from Houston to Washington and then boarded the 'Trooper' that flies three times a week from Washington to RAF Brize Norton in Oxfordshire. I arrived safely and then travelled to Plymouth, changed my clothes, did some washing, and caught the train back to Brize Norton for the flight down to Gibraltar. I must have slept a good while on the aircraft because I arrived in Gibraltar feeling very refreshed and caught a taxi to the wardroom in *HMS Rook,* the naval barracks and administrative centre in Gibraltar. Later, a gentleman in 'civvies' said to me: 'I was going to have a word with you on the aircraft, but you were fast asleep.' He was my new squadron captain, Captain Baker. I apologised profusely, but he was a lovely man and would hear no more about it. We had drinks and dined together that night. He was in Gibraltar because *Apollo* was to become part of the 7th Frigate Squadron and he was attending the commissioning ceremony that took place the next day. It was good to see so many of the of the ship's company that I had known during my previous time on board *Ariadne.* The commissioning ceremony duly completed, I flew back into Brize Norton to go down to *HMS Drake,* unload my kit and have a few days' leave.

My time in the Royal Navy was coming to its close. I had signed up for a four-year short service commission and the four years were up in April. As it happens most of 'my ships' were in for refit. Captain Baker, who I'd met in Gibraltar, was the commanding officer of *HMS Argonaut* as well as Captain F7. *Argonaut* was coming to the end of a refit which was the longest in modern times, five years!

The refit took place in Devonport dockyard and I called on him while the ship was being refitted. I was escorted up and down wooden ladders and it seemed to me that there was such a lot left to do. Appearances were deceptive and within a couple of months *Argonaut* was recommissioned on 22 March 1980.

All my ships were now in refit because *Berwick* had

returned from her service as Belize's guard ship and was in for a refit; *Antelope* too, so my programme was confined to the dockyard and *HMS Drake*. Visiting the ships was confined to normal working hours because most people went home in the evenings and the ships were empty of personnel. In a way, it seemed a fitting end to my time as a squadron chaplain.

Many of my parishioners were living in the wardroom of *HMS Drake*, so we saw quite a lot of one another. Indeed, the wardroom of *Berwick,* with whom I had started my sea time, decided to treat me to a meal in the impressive dining hall of the wardroom. Portsmouth had Nelson and Plymouth had Drake, so the walls featured wooden cut outs of the Defeat of the Armada. Dining by candlelight was a very emotional experience for me. My colleagues presented me with a book, signed by all of them. I treasure it to his day, *The Poems of Robbie Burns.*

One of the last things that I had to do was attend the recommissioning of the *Argonaut* in my capacity as squadron chaplain. I was really a 'bag carrier' because the service was conducted by the Chaplain of the Fleet, Ven Basil O'Farrell. There were representatives of the other denominations taking part, but the Chaplain of the Fleet carried out the blessing and that day was the last of my official duties.

Just after *Argonaut*'s recommissioning there was a ceremony in St. Nicholas' Church *HMS Drake* at which the Ven Basil O'Farrell handed over the role of Archdeacon to the Royal Navy and Chaplain of the Fleet to Ray Roberts, my friend and mentor. That evening I was privileged to buy them both a drink. Neither of them were pleased that I was leaving the Royal Navy which was very flattering to say the least. In fact, Basil said, 'You'll be back.' Ray Roberts who was even more unhappy, told me that I would be appointed chaplain to *HMS Cambria,* the South Wales Division of the Royal Naval 33 Reserve based in Cardiff. Its current chaplain was Godfrey Hilliard, who had been in college with me; our paths criss-crossed from time to time. He left *Cambria* and the parish of Whitchurch in Cardiff to join the Royal Navy and I left the Royal Navy to become the parish priest of Beguildy with Heyope in Radnorshire. I was to travel to and from my parish to the RNR for more than twenty years.

My mind now turned to thoughts of parish life which is what I really wanted. I would be back with my family and children whom I missed terribly. The parish was a very rural one and I was looking forward to the challenge. It would be so different to my experience in the Navy.

I officially left the Royal Navy on 27 April 1980, but in reality, because of foreign and sea service leave, I left at the beginning of April. I was sad to leave and as I handed in my ID card and car pass at the regulating office, the chief petty officer said: 'Oh, a brave man going outside.' He was right because the navy is a family. It's a safe and secure job as jobs go and there is great deal of friendship and camaraderie to be had within its 'walls'. I had thoroughly enjoyed my time in the Royal Navy. There had been times of boredom; there had been times of danger and angst, but overall, it was something I would never forget.

What I didn't know was Basil O'Farrell's prophecy would come true: one day I would be coming back.

Acknowledgements

Rob Fulton is an extremely busy man so I would like to thank him for taking the time to prepare the foreword which sets the tone throughout.

I suppose the reason for this book is my grandson. I am very old and he is very young and it is unlikely that I will see him grow to manhood, so I just wanted to let him know about a part of my life which is still important to me, and the idea grew.

So I am grateful to a number of people who helped and guided me with advice and constructive criticism. First, there is Tim Chapman, who read, listened and talked through the early attempts. Next, came Stephanie Chilman who has borne the brunt of the work, whose guidance and suggestions have been outstanding. Then there's my sister-in-law Philippa who steered me towards her friend Stephanie. But always there is my wife Laura, without whose encouragement, patience and tolerance this narrative would never have been begun or completed.

I hope that you like the cover as it was designed by a young and upcoming illustrator, Bogna Zegradzka to whom I am very grateful. We wanted to make this book appear as a fun read and we hope we have achieved this.

Thank you too for reading this book, I hope you find it of interest. It is of course based on memory, so any errors are mine and mine alone.

Finally, I thank the men and women whose lives I shared and whose company I very much enjoyed. They have brought the memories back to life. My grateful thanks to the Royal Navy not only for employing me but for the kind permission to use the photographs of the ships and the crest.

Printed in Great Britain
by Amazon

72926926R00123